# Perilous Journey:

## Memoir of a Bible Smuggler

# *Perilous Journey:*

## *Memoir of a Bible Smuggler*

### Deborah
### Kaine Thompson

For information please direct emails to: kaine@e-maginativewriting.com
Visit our website: e-maginativewriting.com

Printed in the United States of America, 2017

ISBN: 978-0-9856956-8-2

*This book is dedicated to*

*Brother Andrew's Open Doors International*

*and to the Romanian Christians*

*who received and spread God's Word*

*and to Christians worldwide*

*who are persecuted for their faith.*

*God is faithful.*

# Table of Contents

# PREFACE

This is a true story, a chronicle of the greatest adventure of my life, a testament to modern miracles and how obedience to God can "move mountains." In my case, our clandestine trip helped bring down a corrupt and repressive government.

No one is too insignificant, too young, or "not Christian enough" to be used by God for His purposes. All He needs is for you to answer His call. I know because He called me and sent me to bring Bibles to Romanian Christians.

I have tried many times over the years to write this memoir about smuggling Bibles into Romania during the Cold War, but I didn't feel equal to the challenge of capturing the many inexplicable occurrences that my husband and I lived through.

If what we experienced were not actual miracles—the intervention of God in human events—then perfect coincidences happened over and over at just the right times and left us unscathed in a dangerous country where we could have lost our freedom, if not our lives.

Perhaps you don't know the term "Iron Curtain." It is a term that struck fear in the hearts of every American from the forties to the eighties. After World War II, the Soviet Union (Union of Soviet Socialist Republics) consolidated its communist power and created a political, military, and ideological barrier to keep out Western influence.

Winston Churchill, Britain's prime minister, is credited with using the term "Iron Curtain" to describe what was happening in eastern Europe or the Eastern Bloc. The physical manifestation of this barrier was the Berlin Wall, a concrete wall that divided Germany, with democracy in the west and communism in the east.

The period of tension that existed between the West (US and NATO countries) and the East (the Soviet Union and its allies in the Warsaw Pact) was known as the Cold War. The countries in the Warsaw Pact were Albania, Bulgaria, Czechoslovakia, Hungary, East Germany, Poland, Yugoslavia, and Romania. Each of these Communist countries had varying levels of repression.

It was a time of fear, suspicion, and intractable politics. American children who grew up in the fifties and sixties remember monthly nuclear bomb drills in school, crouching under desks or filing downstairs to a bomb shelter with an ominous black and yellow sign. We knew those bombs would be coming from our enemy, the Soviet Union.

After more than thirty years, it is a wonder I remember this trip as vividly as I do. Some things are crystal clear as if they had happened last week; and some are mere glimpses.

Every day as I wrote this book I asked the Lord to give me the knowledge to recall these amazing events. At night, I dreamed. In the morning, I remembered. During the day, I wrote and the words flowed. The more I wrote, the clearer my memories became. It is an adventure that I will never forget.

For the most part, I have written everything down exactly as it happened, but I admit to taking some creative license in recalling conversations. This memoir is as I remember it; with minor alterations in dialogue, and in some cases, the names of the people we met. I have tried to be faithful to my memories, to write what I remembered, and to be true to the One who sent us.

As I researched Romania over the past few years, I was amazed at how things have changed since 1977. At that time, one of our mission goals was to return with a map of the country (unfortunately we were not able to find one). Today, through Google Earth® I was able to view the exact spot where we crossed the Romanian border, see Bucharest with all its roads, buildings, and rivers, and get directions from one part of the country to another.

Other notable changes are that the "Iron Curtain" has literally fallen; the Berlin Wall was torn down in 1989 and people all over the world own little chunks of it. Yugoslavia is no more, and Romania is a free, democratic country. This would have seemed impossible in 1977. Through Brother Andrew's ministry, Open Doors International, and the prayers of countless Christians, the Iron Curtain was torn asunder by weapons of "mass construction."

Truth, not weapons, can change culture. The faith of Christian warriors persecuted in Communist countries was more powerful than ideology. Today, Open Doors continues to reach out to the persecuted church, but now it is to our Christian family in Iran, Syria, Sudan, Colombia, Vietnam and China.

When I began writing this memoir, our country was in an economic meltdown which began with the sub-prime mortgage fiasco and spread to the rest of the world. Many large banks, lending institutions, and insurance companies failed. The stock market lost thirty-four percent of its value. Major companies closed their doors. People all over the country lost their homes to foreclosure. Companies began letting employees go. Unemployment was the worst since the postwar era. Millions of people were out of work and the American culture was abruptly changed.

With America teetering on an economic precipice, the worst economic climate since 1939, Israel and Palestine were at each other's throats, and radical elements saw an opportunity to increase the chaos.

This dire situation persists to this day. Everywhere there are signs of trouble. 'Wars and rumors of wars' abound. Terrorism is no longer something "over there." It strikes in France, in England, in America, at restaurants, publishing companies, vacation resorts, schools, and even intersections. Nowhere is safe. No one is "safe". Everyone you talk to seems nervous, worried, and scared. Our world seems to be shaking at its foundation. The norms have been shattered and everyone is looking for answers.

Where do we find these answers? We must look beyond ourselves. Cynicism is the new norm. Crazy theories and religions have popped up with some elements of truth hidden in new, more palatable packaging. People prefer to say that they are "spiritual," and that "the universe" will meet their needs, rather than acknowledge God's sovereign power.

For too many, God is nothing more than a comforting concept for the weak-minded and desperate. Our sophisticated society puts its faith in science and momentary delights. Spiritual matters have been relegated to discussions of UFOs, reincarnation, Eastern philosophies, ghosts, zombies, vampires, and psychics; but they only pose questions, they do not provide answers.

God is the answer. God is welcoming to all who seek His ways.

# CHAPTER 1

## Washing Windows

It is often in the mundane tasks of life that revelation comes. For me, the task was washing windows.

It was 1977. I was twenty-four years old and living in a mansion in Leusden, Holland, the culmination of many prayers and miracles. The ceiling of our three-room apartment on the third floor was twelve feet high. The windows were arched and narrow with heavy working shutters on either side. To wash each windowpane, I had to open the adjoining window, sit on the sill, hold onto the center strut, lean out as far as I could and clean the dusty exterior.

I wanted the windows to be clear because the view from my apartment was spectacular. From the living room window, I could look out over the expanse of the grand lawn to acres of the dense forest beyond. Peacocks, wild swans, and deer were often in view, feeding on the grass. Several paths led away from the house through a forest of majestic beech trees, which rose from eighty to a hundred feet. At night, stars glittered in a clear sky and the moon shone through the windows.

Once, from these tall, arched windows, I witnessed the culling of wild hares in an age-old ceremony, which was done to prepare provisions for the winter months. My attention was initially caught by the blare of the ceremonial horn, signaling the start of the culling. The hunters gathered below in the parking lot. They were dressed in leather jerkins, green flannel vests, and grey breeches, with their shotguns tucked under their arms. I saw them march into the forest to take up their shooting positions.

The villagers gathered below to serve as beaters. They spread out in a line and walked into the forest, beating on drums and metal pipes to scare the game toward the hunters. As wild hares and grouse fled before the beaters, the hunters began to pick them off in an endless volley of bullets. The game warden followed afterward and strung up the dead animals on a wheeled teepee-like cart. The culling went on all afternoon.

I was continually fascinated by other scenes I saw from those arched windows so high above the ground: a herd of timid roe deer on the lawn, wild boar trotting past and disappearing under the brush, peacocks strutting and pecking, often shrieking "help" in the night, scaring me to death, and my children and their little friends playing chasing games, shouting with delight. These visual wonders must be observed through clean, clear glass.

The soapy pail of water was at my feet. I thrust the sponge into the water, squeezed out the excess, and prepared myself for the task.

With bubbles rising up my arm, soaking my sleeve, I grabbed the center strut with my hand, swung my upper body out and reached the opposite window with my sponge. I began scrubbing a winter's worth of grime off the windowpane. I scrubbed vigorously, intent on removing every piece of dirt that might impede my view.

"Look down." A voice spoke.

I looked down. The gravel parking lot was more than forty feet below. It was as if each small pebble became magnified, I was seeing them as if plunging toward them. For a brief second, in my mind's eye, I saw myself falling and hitting the ground, lying crumpled and flattened on the gravel below. The ground came in and out of focus. I felt dizzy. I gasped. My gut contracted. With one slip of my soapy hand, I could fall and die.

"Have no fear. I have you in the palm of my hand. Follow me and nothing will harm you."

I knew immediately who spoke. It was the voice of God.

The words rang in my ears. My heart drummed in my chest. I quickly pulled back into the apartment, placed my hands on the sill and looked down, breathing heavily. It was a long way. I shook all over. Not from the narrow escape of my potential death, but from the certainty that God had spoken aloud—spoken to me. Even after all these years, when I recall this moment, the words clang like cymbals and I remember His voice. It is unlike any other.

As a Christian believer, I expected to hear from God. I prayed every night and often during the day; little prayers saying "help me with this," or "forgive me for that," or "please open a way for me to make a difference." I heard God in my head, like my conscience, confirming my faith. But this was not that. This was a real voice, come unbidden into the air.

*Have no fear. I have you in the palm of my hand. Follow me and nothing will harm you.*

My ears literally hurt from the sound as if the still, small voice of God was more a sonic boom than a whisper.

Stunned, I looked out over the wooded landscape that surrounded the mansion, waiting for my heart to slow down. I took a deep breath. The sight was pastoral, peaceful, and I was so thankful to be living in this beautiful place that God had made possible.

The sound of my children squealing with joy and the thump of my husband's footsteps rushing up the narrow stairs to our apartment and into the living room pulled me from my reverie. I had only just recovered from my experience of hearing God's voice.

"Honey. You won't believe it," my husband Lon said. "Sit down. I've got some news."

"What is it?" I asked, sitting on the couch. He joined me, as did the boys, squirming onto my lap.

"We got one. Brother Andrew has given us a mission."

My husband's radiant face exhibited none of the queasiness that filled my stomach and the trepidation of what those words meant. The mission he was so excited about was to smuggle Bibles to where the strong and fearless feared to tread.

Brother Andrew started Open Doors Ministry[1] and made his first daring trip behind the Iron Curtain in 1955. I am happy to say that his ministry continues to this day by those who believe with all their hearts that there are no closed doors to God's Word.

His mission has always been simple. Wherever the Word of God is denied, Open Doors will smuggle Bibles, Christian literature, and songbooks to the persecuted church so that godless nations would be overthrown not by guns, but through prayer and songs of praise. Simple, right?

"No kidding," I said, squeezing his hand for reassurance. "He chose us? How exciting. Where to? Poland? Estonia? Czechoslovakia?"

"Romania," he said, checking my reaction, but I was ignorant.

"Romania? Where's that?"

"Next to Yugoslavia."

"Oh. Yugoslavia is supposed to be friendly to Westerners."

"Uh, honey, it's not like Yugoslavia. In fact, you need to know that it's the most oppressive regime behind the Iron Curtain. Open Doors hasn't been able to get any missions through since Brother Andrew went in the fifties. Four failed attempts, so far. The underground church is being persecuted in terrible ways. I'm afraid it is a very dangerous place."

"It is?" My stomach fluttered with apprehension.

My husband persisted, seeing my reaction. "They said we are an answer to prayer."

I looked at my two boys, nestled under my arms. Four-year-old Nathan stared intently into his father's face, trying to figure out what was being said. Three-year-old Eli put his arms around my neck, responding to my mood change.

"But we've never done anything like this before," I said, searching his eyes for doubt. "Why would they send us to such a dangerous place? If no one has ever made it across, how are we going to do it? Are you sure they said Romania? Maybe that's just a suggestion."

"They said Romania. They believe that because we're Americans we have the best chance for success. They want us to pray about it and get back to them. What should I tell them? Should we answer the call?"

A million thoughts flashed in my head. I was having a hard time absorbing his words. Romania! The most repressive Communist country in Eastern Europe! That's where they wanted us to go on our first mission? It was crazy. Madness. How could we do this? What if we got caught?

*Have no fear. I have you in the palm of my hand.*

The words boomed in my ears. Was I going to give in to fear or believe?

*Follow me and nothing will harm you.*

God had already spoken to me, preparing me for this moment. His church was crying out to Him. Why else would He have spoken? He would not let anything happen to us. Whether I was doing the work of God or washing windows forty feet above ground, He held my life in His hands.

I had no more doubt. I nodded my assent, bundled my children into my arms and thanked God that we had been chosen for this dangerous mission to the persecuted church in Romania.

"We will go," I said with certainty.

"We don't have to worry," Lon said, hugging me and crushing the children in our embrace. "God is on our side. I'll call Brother Andrew right now. We're supposed to leave in two weeks."

He jumped up and ran down to the first floor to the only phone in the mansion. There was no turning back now. We were about to do what no one else had done since Brother Andrew—smuggle Bibles into the very heart of Romania.

# CHAPTER 2

# A Far Cry from Vietnam

Five years earlier, I would have been shocked to think I would volunteer for a dangerous mission smuggling Bibles behind the Iron Curtain, much less go through with it. I was not a brave person. I was just an average American military wife, raising a family and trusting in God for a modest livelihood.

In 1972, I was nineteen, a young mother with a little baby and was pregnant again. The Vietnam War was still going strong. The country was in turmoil. Anti-war demonstrations were becoming more violent. Vietnam vets had thrown their medals onto the Capitol steps. The draft had sucked the life out of America's young male population, eventually killing 58,000 soldiers, and disillusionment and fear were pervasive.

Even the clergy had taken to raiding draft boards and forming human chains around federal courthouses to protest the trial of Father Daniel Berrigan for his anti-war activities. Students across the country broke into university buildings to stage "sit-ins" to protest the escalation of bombing in North Vietnam.

Despite this, President Richard Nixon was re-elected, and it looked as if the war would never end. As an artist and part-time construction worker, my husband Lon was in danger of being drafted. Even though the government was drawing down the number of troops in Vietnam, the draft went inexorably on and his "number" would soon be up.

Not wanting to be drafted, which would guarantee his deployment to Vietnam, he enlisted in the U.S. Air Force. He scored high in electronics and, after six weeks of basic training in San Antonio, Texas, was sent to avionics school in Rantoul, Illinois.

While he trained, the baby inside me grew. I spent my time running after an active one-year-old, keeping our rented trailer house clean, making meals and watching the Watergate hearings on television. I was riveted by the startling testimony. I knew I was watching history in the making.

A week before my due date, my husband received his orders to report to George Air Force Base in Victorville, California. He was to be at Commander's Call on the date I was due to give birth. It was a dilemma. I would have to stay in Illinois while he went to California and then wait six months before the baby and I could travel by airplane to California. Or, I could give birth now. I guzzled a bottle of castor oil (a folk remedy not recommended) and went into labor the next morning. Our second son, Eli, was born in Urbana, Illinois. Three days later we drove nonstop to California.

Once we were settled, I was horrified to learn that the majority of the airmen at George Air Force Base were being deployed to Thailand or Vietnam. I met many Air Force wives caring for their children alone, living in constant fear for their mates working in the war zones and knew that it was only a matter of time before I was one of them. I prayed continually that Lon would be sent somewhere else.

When his orders came through our jaws dropped. He was to report to Soesterberg Air Base in Soest, Holland for the remainder of his duty. While everyone else was going to Thailand or Vietnam, we were going to Holland—the land of dikes, flowers and wooden shoes! What a great place to raise my children.

Nathan was two and Eli was one when we moved to Amersfoort, Holland. The American government had sold several new F-4E jets to the Dutch and provided avionic specialists from the U.S. Air Force to maintain their existing F-4 Phantoms. The planes rarely needed maintenance so the biggest challenge most airmen faced was boredom.

Lon spent many happy days painting a mural on the wall of the avionics room—the flight of the Kitty Hawk—or designing and painting personalized wooden shoes as goodbye gifts for departing Air Force personnel. As word spread about his art, more and more requests came in from high-ranking officers. On the silver anniversary of Holland's Queen Juliana's coronation, Camp Soesterberg presented her with a gift of my husband's personalized wooden shoes.

We had many three-day passes and used the time to travel

throughout Europe. We bought a Volkswagen bus and converted it into a camper. Our children became great travelers.

After eight months in Holland, we discovered an American church near Soesterberg Air Base. It was not a regular kind of church. The Good News Christian Fellowship met in a two-story house in the quaint neighborhood of Den Dolder. The church was founded by the Reverend Walter Jones, an elderly, down-home, American Baptist preacher and his wife, Ann, who had made it their mission to provide for the spiritual needs of American airmen at Soesterberg Air Base. This wonderful couple opened their home to young servicemen and couples like us.

Their house had a large living room where we met for services, and a good-sized yard where our children played. The church was like being in America, where good, old-fashioned hymns led by Rev. Jones's booming voice and a warm hug from Ann made everyone feel at home. When we first went to the church there were twenty people meeting regularly. We met on Sunday for celebration service, Tuesday for Bible study, Friday for music and worship, and any day of the week when prayer or counseling was needed. Rev. Jones and his wife were a source of comfort and spiritual guidance.

It was not easy, particularly for the young airmen, to avoid some of Holland's more liberal opportunities. Prostitution was sanctioned and regulated by the government. Drug use was frowned upon, but there was little police enforcement. Select cafes in Amsterdam offered a variety of marijuana blends for sale and potent hashish was freely transported from Morocco. Amsterdam was the end of the Poppy Trail from Afghanistan. It was a place of free delights and distractions, but ultimately it led to many ruined lives or a rude awakening for those in the American military who were caught. For many of the American servicemen, this was the first time they had been away from home and the temptations were legion.

A year after we joined the church, Reverend Jones announced that he and Ann would be returning to the States as soon as they could find a replacement. We felt like we were losing our grandparents. Reverend Jones brought in a young Dutch pastor, Reverend Hans Cornelder, and his American wife, Cheryl, to take over the ministry. As the Joneses went back to the States, the Cornelders moved in and GNCF was never the same.

Where the Joneses had provided a comfortable family environment, the Cornelders brought youthfulness, modern music, excitement, and an evangelistic fervor that lit a fire in everyone who came.

As more and more Americans and Dutch families heard about GNCF, it became harder and harder to find a place to sit in the large living room. Hans delivered profound, moving sermons and Cheryl, with her beautiful voice, led us in worship that could transport us to heavenly realms. I learned many deep and lasting lessons during this time.

One lesson, in particular, comes to mind. We were all challenged by the arrival into our congregation of the base screw-up; a pudgy, myopic guy who not only had run a forklift into an F-18 but ruined his own car just because he forgot to put oil into it. When he bought a moped, he ran it into one of the Queen's trees and by Dutch law had to pay for the tree's repair. We were constantly taking up collections to help him out. His wife was equally problematic.

She was extremely overweight and had a terrible body odor. Once they arrived, it was difficult to enjoy our Bible studies because the smell was overpowering. They were very sweet people, but they were socially repellent. People started to complain because of the woman's body odor and the frequency of collections to bail them out.

One Sunday, Hans gave a sermon on Matthew 5:32, 36: "If you love those who love you, what thanks do you deserve? Why even sinners love those who love them. If you do good to those who do good to you, what thanks do you deserve? Even sinners do that. Be merciful, just as your Father is merciful."

He told us that as Christians we are called to love the unlovable. What does it say about us if we love only those who are "acceptable" to us? We are no different from those who don't know God's love. God sees our hearts. We are called to be like Jesus. Are we to reject those who make us uncomfortable or are we to welcome them as Jesus would?

We were all convicted in our hearts for our bad feelings and unkind comments about the couple. The women of GNCF decided to help the woman with her odor problem, and the men decided to help the guy with his accident proneness and financial problems. These were not easy tasks.

These kind, loving people just didn't fit in. It was difficult and embarrassing to talk to the woman about her odor, but she took it well. It turned out that she had a physical condition, not an aversion to showering. We got her to the base doctor and he prescribed her some medication, which took care of the odor.

The men intervened to keep their comrade from causing accidents and helped him budget his finances. They would always be "different," but we learned to love them as they were. They flourished under the care of the church.

GNCF continued to grow. The lovely and unlovely sat side-by-side, wall-to-wall, and worshiped together. It got so full that we began to use the dining room as well, leaving the door open so those in the overflow could hear the sermon. Many American families, as well as some of the Dutch, came for the service and stayed for the day. Eventually, we began to have potlucks after church, with everyone bringing a dish to share (the single servicemen brought the soft drinks).

Led by Reverend Cornelder, we began praying for a larger place to hold our church services. It was a new concept for many of us. It was much easier to pray for things in the abstract than things in the specific. I often prayed for peace in Vietnam, to be a good mother, to be loving to my husband, etc., but the idea that God would answer specific prayer requests was new to many of us.

One night in a regular prayer meeting, the pastor's wife, Cheryl, received a powerful vision that would change all of our lives. She spoke with such authority that I believed something supernatural had happened. She said she saw a big square white house with long green shutters that would be our new church. She said that it would be surrounded by a moat.

I muffled a giggle when I heard that, figuring she was embellishing on a good idea. A moat. Right. That pretty much narrowed down our possibilities. Then someone else had a word of knowledge and said we would know this house by all the scriptures on the walls.

Oh, come on, I thought. A big house with a moat around it and full of scriptural graffiti. If they got any more specific we'd never find a place to hold our services.

At another prayer meeting, we were again praying for our new place. We were bursting at the seams and didn't know what to do. I was praying fervently, hoping that Holy Spirit would speak to me as He had to Cheryl and others. Just after I thought these words, I had a vision. It was as clear as a remembered dream.

I saw a great meadow filled with sheep of many colors. Only the sheep were lying on their sides as if dead. Just then, over the hill came many soldiers in battle gear. They poured over the field and each went to a sheep and breathed into its mouth. The sheep were revived, stood up and began to eat. Although I was scared to speak about this, I told everyone what I saw.

Someone spoke, I can't remember whom, and interpreted the vision. They said the house would be a place where American soldiers would be used to revive "lost sheep," those who were spiritually bankrupt or wounded by persecution; those who had lost their faith or never known the love of our living God. People of many nations would come together to be revived and healed because this house would be a house of peace. Everyone was convinced that this would be the purpose of the house and our ministry. I was amazed and humbled that my vision was seen as an answer to prayer.

Intellectually I knew that we needed a larger place, but I was new to believing that God could speak directly to His people. I learned to have faith that God was going to bring this about. I learned that I could also be used by God if I had the courage to speak out. I learned to listen for God's voice and be ready to encourage the Body of Christ.

As we waited several months for the fulfillment of what we took to be God's outrageous promises, our prayers and active faith were the beginning of many spiritual lessons for our church.

# CHAPTER 3

# The Shalom House

The members of our church looked for the big white square house for many months. Everyone who attended GNCF drove around the local villages and scanned the houses for the one described in the vision. We even went to real estate offices with a sketch Cheryl had drawn of the house in the vision. They thought we were crazy. Some members of the church began to lose faith in our spiritual house hunting process.

After many months of searching and praying, we found it.

Huize Den Boom (House of Trees) was located in the village of Leusden, only ten kilometers from Soesterberg Air Base. It was a real mansion: white, square, with tall green shutters. It looked just like Cheryl's sketch from her vision.

Around the house was a large, dense forest and, believe it or not, a moat. The only way to get to the mansion was to cross the moat over a small brick bridge and go up a long driveway. Behind the house was a huge gravel parking lot of white stone that would accommodate many cars for Sunday service. It was perfect in every way. We were convinced this was the house in the vision. There wasn't one of us who had a twinge of doubt that such a magnificent building could become our new church. Every night for weeks, one of the members of our church would stand at the bridge to Huize Den Boom and claim it for the Lord.

Upon further investigation, we learned that the house belonged to Dutch royalty—the Baroness de Beaufort who had recently died. It was managed by wealthy trustees who met quarterly in a room on the second floor—locked to all but them. We were all very curious about that room.

Our spirits leaped for joy to learn that the trustees were in the process of accepting applications for tenants, but they weren't just accepting anyone who could pay the rent. In her will, the Baroness had stipulated that Huize Den Boom was to be used only for Christian purposes to heal the land and the people devastated by war. It was to be a place of peace.

We quickly expressed our interest and applied for tenancy. Within a month, the trustees contacted us that they had decided that the Good News Christian Fellowship fulfilled the wishes of the Baroness de Beaufort. We would become the new tenants.

Imagine our amazement when we entered the house through the huge oak doors, inset with intricate stained glass, to find Bible verses on every wall, just as the prophecy had foretold. As the trustee explained, the Baroness had been bedridden for many years and occupied her time by embroidering scriptures. When she finished one she would have it framed and hung on the wall and then begin another one. These embroidered scriptures filled the walls throughout the mansion. Where once I had doubted, I now believed. My faith grew.

We called our new home the Shalom House because it was a house of peace. Everyone who wanted to live in the house was allowed to put forth their name. It was agreed that the whole church would pray about who would become the live-in tenants. Many people wanted to live in a mansion. Because we had two young children, I didn't think we would be selected. But we were.

We moved into Huize Den Boom with two other families and four single American servicemen. The other two couples were Steph and Diane DeJong and Reverend Hans and Cheryl Cornelder. The young airmen were Al, Chris, Ryan, and Jake. We all agreed on the rental contract.

It was also decided that Sandy, a young, Mennonite *au pair* from Kansas, would live rent-free. In return, she would serve as the first-floor housekeeper and chef for our weekly, communal "love feasts" on Saturdays and our after Sunday service congregational luncheons.

Sandy proved to be a culinary genius at creating delicious soups to feed hundreds of people after church. I can still see her in the kitchen in front of the monstrous industrial stove, stirring the soups in two giant kettles. The ladies of the house, including me, had the responsibility of peeling and chopping the ingredients for the soup and making hundreds of peanut butter and jelly, cheese, and tomato sandwiches. It was one of my favorite tasks.

The Cornelder and DeJong children were the same ages as my own. They were Anita and Daniel DeJong and Amy and David Cornelder. Imagine six small children, ages three to five, roaming that massive house and its soccer field-sized lawns. With all the servicemen who lived there, they were never without adult supervision or attention.

Each floor had twelve-foot ceilings and gorgeous marble fireplaces in almost every room. A wide wooden staircase connected the three floors. The balustrade was solid white oak polished to a glossy sheen. The children loved to play on the landings between floors and on the wide wooden steps.

Other than Sandy's apartment, the first floor of the mansion was open to the public and used for our communal gatherings. The largest room served as our sanctuary. This floor also included the kitchen, laundry, solarium/library and dining room. The second floor was the living quarters for the Cornelder and DeJong families. The Thompsons and the single men lived on the third floor. The four airmen from Camp Soesterberg shared a large communal room outfitted with bunk beds.

My apartment on the third floor had a living room/kitchen and two bedrooms. Our furniture looked puny in the massive rooms with their twelve-foot ceilings. The only drawback to our setup was that in this sprawling mansion there were only two bathrooms (water closets), one on the first floor and one on the second floor; there was none on the third floor where I lived. The second-floor bathroom was a double-seater. I couldn't understand the purpose of that, except to accommodate two children. Unfortunately, it was connected to the only bathing room.

The lack of bathrooms was a challenge for Americans who were used to accessible and private facilities. Those living on the third floor: myself, my husband, my children and four grown men, had to run down the big staircase to the bathroom. I began to employ the European custom of using a chamber pot whenever possible.

The second floor contained the only bathing facility. It was a large, tiled room with a deep claw-foot ceramic tub with a handheld spray nozzle. With so many people living in the house, we had to schedule our bathing times, and if someone was bathing, the second-floor bathroom was unavailable. The only toilet left was the water closet on the first floor. There was also only one rotary phone on the first floor. When it rang, the stairs thundered with footsteps as the airmen raced to get there first.

According to the Baroness's will, the tenants were to have access to the entire estate, except for one room on the second floor, which was reserved for the trustees of the estate. Only once was I privileged to enter this secret boardroom. Before their quarterly board meeting, the trustees requested coffee and cakes and asked if the women of the house could serve them. Cheryl, Diane, Sandy and I readily accepted the job.

As we entered with our trays of coffee and cakes, our mouths dropped open. The room was filled end-to-end with a large, highly polished ebony table; its edges were elaborately inlaid with mother of pearl. The matching ebony chairs were overstuffed and comfortable, looking like thrones.

The walls were floor to ceiling shelves, filled with rare books, sculptures, and priceless antiques. I was particularly drawn to the collection of antique music boxes on one side of the room. The metal disks for the larger music boxes were three feet in diameter and could play for an hour. Rare and beautiful things filled every nook and cranny, making the room look like an antique shop rather than a boardroom. As I set my tray of cakes on the table, I inhaled the exotic mixture of espresso, old books, tobacco, linseed oil, and cedar that filled the room.

Another stipulation of the will was that Baroness de Beaufort's butler would live out his life on the estate. His name was Meneer Van Asselt. He was an old man, tall and lean, and very kind. I learned most of my conversational Dutch from him.

Oftentimes, when the ladies of the house gathered to peel potatoes and vegetables for the communal luncheon we offered on Sundays, Meneer Van Asselt would sit with us and tell amazing stories about his life as a butler in the house. Although Cheryl translated his words, I was eager to learn the language to hear what he had to say when she wasn't there to translate. Gradually I began to pick up enough phrases and words that I could follow his recollections.

He loved to talk to us. He would come into the kitchen for coffee, and then pull up a chair to the table. We always had a cookie ready for him. He told us thrilling stories about how the de Beauforts fled their home as the Nazis invaded Holland during World War II. The Nazis confiscated Huize Den Boom and used it as their headquarters. Throughout the war, Meneer Van Asselt and his father hid out on the land and watched over Huize Den Boom until the liberation of Holland by American forces. It was a great day when the Baroness and her family returned to their beloved home as peace returned to Holland.

Meneer Van Asselt's father, grandfather, and great-grandfather had all served as butlers for the family de Beaufort. I still remember the former butler walking across the lawn or bicycling in his wooden shoes, or *klompen*, as he continued to watch over the land. He was a lovely, generous man. Before I left Holland, he gave me a set of hand-blown crystal icicles that I hang every year on my Christmas tree to remember his kindness.

As we settled into our impressive new home, our congregation grew exponentially. We had more than a hundred people attending every Sunday. At the end of the service, the entire congregation was invited to the soup and sandwich luncheon set up outside on the expansive lawns.

People often spent the whole day at the Shalom House. They played football, badminton, Frisbee, and croquet; or put together "jamming sessions" for everyone who played an instrument, mostly guitars, recorders, harmonicas, and bongos. Walking through the forest on the many trails was also a favorite Sunday pastime. An atmosphere of peace prevailed.

Word spread about the growing church. An entire network of Christians began to share the remarkable story of the founding of the Shalom House. People came from all over Europe to attend our Sunday services and to stay for the soup and sandwich feast afterward. Close friends of Princess Beatrix of the Netherlands became regular attendees. Many times we were blessed with world-renowned guest speakers.

One of those speakers was the legendary Corrie Ten Boom, whose book *The Hiding Place*[2] was widely read. During World War II, her family hid many Jews who would eventually make it to freedom. Sadly, the Ten Booms were betrayed and imprisoned. Four of Corrie's immediate family died in the concentration camps.[3] Corrie survived the brutal life of Ravensbruck, a notorious death camp, to become a renowned evangelical leader and speaker.

She spoke about what she had endured, and the faith of her sister, Betsie, who died in the camp. As she spoke, she appeared to radiate light. From her gold and silver hair piled up on top her head to her sturdy leather brown Dutch shoes, she glowed.

She told a story I will never forget. She explained that in the previous year she had spoken at a Christian conference in Germany. At the end of the conference, she prayed for people individually. There was an old man who waited in the long line. When he finally stood before her he said, "Do you know who I am?"

She looked at him more closely and realized with a shock that this was the Ravensbruck guard who had sadistically mistreated her sister, eventually causing her death.

"I know you," she said, trying to control her emotions.

"Can you forgive me?" he asked.

"Do you know the Savior?"

"I do," he said, weeping, "and though my sin was great, He forgave me."

"Then, brother, I forgive you, too."

I was stunned by her words. How could she forgive someone who had been so cruel to her and her sister? How could she let him off the hook? Only the grace of God could allow her to forgive a man who had been largely responsible for her sister's death and her own misery.

"There is no pit so deep that God's love is not deeper still," she told us. Her story and spirit filled me with a conviction that I needed to do more for Christ.

Another guest speaker was Brother Andrew from Open Doors Ministry. His 1967 book, *God's Smuggler*[4] had created a sensation among Christians, particularly those in the West who had no conception of the horrific persecution of Christians behind the Iron Curtain.

He didn't look like a smuggler. He was a nice, ordinary Dutch man in his forties. He spoke softly, but his words rang in my ears. His ministry was accomplishing incredible mission work—smuggling Bibles to the persecuted church around the world. He encouraged us to live radically for Jesus Christ. He told us about how God had changed his life and had laid a burden on his heart for the people behind the Iron Curtain. He made his first trip to Yugoslavia in the 1950s, and later traveled to Romania.

He drove to Romania in his little Volkswagen packed with Bibles. At the border, he watched as the guards thoroughly searched and ransacked every car in front of him. He watched as one car was literally taken apart. Faced with certain discovery, he prayed for a miracle. He said, "Lord, I know that no amount of cleverness on my part can get me through this search. Let me take some of the Bibles out and leave them in the open. Then I will be depending utterly upon you." When it was his turn, the border guards looked at his passport and waved him through. The Bibles were on the seat beside him in plain sight of the border guards, but they didn't notice them.

At the end of his message, Lon and I were so moved by his story and the mission of Open Doors that we gave him our information and let him know we were willing to serve as couriers if he ever had a mission for us. We had no idea that he would take us up on our offer or that we would face almost the exact situation at the Romanian border.

"You're going where?" my mother asked when I finally got through to her in Idaho. I could hear the shock in her voice over the phone as she received the news of our mission.

"Romania," I said, praying under my breath. I felt the stunned silence and rushed to fill it. "Don't worry, Mom, we're convinced that God has called us to do this. It will be okay."

"How can you ask me not to worry? I'm your mother. It's what I do." I held my breath, waiting for her repudiation of my faith.

"But before I became your mother, I became a child of God. If He says He wants you to go, I know He will keep you safe—but I'll be assaulting the gates of heaven with my prayers until you get safely back. I'm proud of you. I don't think I could do it."

I nearly cried with relief and love. "I know you could if God called you. Thank you, Mom. I feel so much better knowing you're going to be praying for me."

"Not just me," she said. "I'm putting you on every prayer list I know about. You'll have the prayers of many people. God will be with you both. I even know a senator who will be hearing from me if you have any trouble."

We talked about the children and whether to take them along or not before hanging up. I felt a great heaviness lift from my shoulders. I knew that my mother's prayers and the prayers of everyone she knew would be with us.

# CHAPTER 4

# Preparations

"It's not going to be easy crossing the border," my husband said.

"That goes without saying," I replied, snuggling up next to him on the couch. He put his arm around me and pulled me close.

The children were long in bed and we were on the first floor in the solarium. It was one of our favorite places in the Shalom House. It was an annex attached to the main building. Its roof and one wall were composed of clear glass panels. It was the perfect place to grow indoor plants. Ferns, coleus, spiderwort, philodendron, and ivy grew in pots on plant stands and tables throughout the room.

On the opposite wall was a large bookshelf that held reference material, inspirational books, Bibles, and literature that people had donated. There were even two shelves dedicated to fiction, including murder mysteries, historical novels, thrillers, and innocuous romances. Somebody had donated a nearly complete set of the *Encyclopedia Britannica.*[5]

We were sitting on a wicker couch made more comfortable with fluffy pillows. There were several other wicker chairs on the other side of the room, available for those who liked to sit in the sun and read. We preferred to be there at night when the house was still and the stars shone through the glass.

"I mean it! You don't know how serious this is."

His tone made me look at him. "What is it? What's wrong?"

"Nothing. Forget it. I shouldn't have said that."

"Tell me. Did you learn something I should know?"

My blood ran cold as he told me what one of the Open Doors volunteers had said to him. It was the latest news out of Romania.

"This truck driver had waited so long in line at the border that he was desperate to urinate. He got out of his truck, walked into the bushes to relieve himself and was riddled with bullets from the border guards."

"They killed him because he had to pee?"

"Because he left his truck unexpectedly with the motor running. I guess the command at the Romanian border is shoot first and ask questions later."

The message was clear. The Romanian border was not impossible to cross, but if anything was out of the ordinary or suspicious; we could be detained, imprisoned, or killed without question or cause. We would be smuggling more than a million dollars of contraband across this border. It was cause enough to be imprisoned for life or killed outright.

There was almost no current information coming out of Romania. It was a dark country, cut off from the rest of the world by its government. I tried to find out all I could, but the Iron Curtain was what the term implied—impenetrable, with nothing going in and nothing coming out.

All I was able to learn from the *Encyclopedia Britannica* was what had happened before the Iron Curtain fell. The last entry was the abdication of Romania's King Michael and the signing of the Warsaw Pact in 1955. Romania was now under the brutal regime of Nicolae Ceausescu, General Secretary of the Romanian Communist Party and President of Romania.

I swallowed hard. My mind raced ahead to people telling my children that we were dead. My mother's face filled with grief. My father crying…

"Hey! Where'd you go?" Lon asked, shaking my shoulder.

"It's so terrible. That poor man. His poor family. I guess it never really sank in before what we are about to do."

"I knew I shouldn't have told you."

"No. No, I'm glad you did. What kind of faith do I have if I've got some sugar-coated fantasy to believe in. I needed to hear that. I need to face stark reality. It will make my faith stronger, knowing the danger that we face and God's ability to protect us. Let me tell you what little I've learned from the *Encyclopedia Britannica.*"

I retrieved my notebook that I had left on the table and started reading my notes.

"From what I could find, Romania's history is long and troubled. It was founded way back in the first century as a Roman province. Eastern Orthodox Christianity was established in the eighth century when the Bulgarian Empire absorbed the land. I learned that the Eastern Orthodox Church traces its origins to Christ and the Apostles.

"After the fall of the Roman Empire, the faith spread to Eastern Europe. Over time they split with Roman Catholicism over doctrinal issues, such as the primacy of Catholicism, the nature of the Trinity, and other differences. Anyway, in the eleventh century, the Hungarian Empire snatched up Transylvania, and in the sixteenth century, the country became part of the Ottoman Empire."

"Wait a minute," Lon interrupted, "did you say Transylvania? Like in Count Dracula?"

"You got it. Vlad Dracula was a Wallachian prince in the eighteenth century. He repelled the invading Turkish armies, cut off the heads of his prisoners and impaled them on spikes. Quite grisly. He became a great folk hero and is credited with founding the city of Bucharest. Imagine that!"

"You mean he actually existed?" he asked.

"Not as the author Bram Stoker made him out to be. He wasn't a vampire, but he terrified the Turks. Known as Vlad the Impaler. I thought Transylvania was an imaginary country. Can you believe we're going to the city that Count Dracula founded? Talk about confronting evil. You want me to go on?"

"Yes. This is getting good."

"But sad," I said, and continued with my history lesson. "In the nineteenth century, Romania became a protectorate of Russia. Ironically, this was a time of great cultural renewal and intellectual growth for the country. Universities and opera houses were established. In 1881, the Romanians said 'thanks, but no thanks' to Russia and proclaimed itself a kingdom. In World War I it sided with the Allies, so at the end of the war, it doubled in size. Transylvania was once again made part of the kingdom.

"Unfortunately, this did not improve the lives of the people. King Carol II was crowned in 1938. He formed a royal dictatorship, abolished the constitution and founded a Fascist state. Under pressure from his own Fascist government, he was forced to abdicate and went into exile.

"In World War II, the Romanian Fascists sided with Germany against the Soviet Union. Half of Romania's Jewish population, more than a half million people, were exterminated, as well as most of the Roma."

"Roma? You mean as in Gypsies? Gypsies come from Romania? I didn't know that."

"I was a bit confused by that as well, so I looked it up. They actually originated in East Asia, probably India. There's quite a large population in the Balkan States, including Romania. They've been persecuted throughout the centuries.

"In medieval times, people believed that Gypsies were descended from the mating of a woman and Satan. Another rumor was that the Romany people forged the nails used to crucify Christ. Regardless, they have suffered as a people. During World War II, Himmler ordered their extermination. Only about five thousand survived the death camps."

"Unbelievable. So why is this important?"

"It's not. I just thought it was interesting. Should I go on?" He nodded.

"So, in 1944, King Michael... "

"Wait a minute. Who's King Michael?" Lon asked.

"He was the son of King Carol and a great-great-grandson of Queen Victoria. He was the Crown Prince. Anyway, Michael led a coup and ousted the Fascists. By that time, the Soviet occupation of Romania was almost assured. He signed the armistice and declared war on Germany.

"Under the terms of the armistice, Romania recognized its defeat by the USSR and was placed under occupation of the Allied forces with the Soviets in control of the country—a bad move. If only we'd known what that would mean to Eastern Europe. By 1947, the king was forced to abdicate and go into exile as the Communists came to power. In 1955, Romania joined the Warsaw Pact, and the Iron Curtain closed off all communication. That's about it."

"But what about Ceausescu? Wasn't there anything in there about his rise to power?"

"Nothing. The entries all end with the Warsaw Pact. All that it said is that the Communists are now in control."

"Well, hopefully, we'll get some inside information from Open Doors. But I'm afraid we'll be going into the country blind."

"Given its history, I don't expect we'll find happy people living there," I said, closing my notebook. We both sat quietly, each pondering the mission we had accepted.

"Well, we'll be bringing them rivers of living water for their thirsty souls," Lon said, taking my hand in his.

"That's beautiful. You're right. It's good that we're doing this, isn't it?"

"Yes, darling, it is. We are an answer to prayer, and that's a fact. I just wish we knew more about what we were facing."

"Maybe tomorrow when you meet with Open Doors. It's late. Let's get some sleep."

The next day, Lon received further information on our mission. Brother Andrew's representative prayed fervently with him. He did not sugarcoat the risks. Once we crossed the Romanian border, we would be on our own. If we were discovered, we could expect imprisonment and possibly death. They tried to reassure him that since we were Americans, there was a good chance that we wouldn't just "disappear." They suggested that we inform as many of our Christian and political friends in America as we could about our mission plans.

Much of what Open Doors knew about what was going on in Romania came from the testimony of Richard Wurmbrand[6], a Romanian Messianic Jew, known as the "voice of the underground church." He spent almost nine years in prison, three in solitary confinement, and was repeatedly tortured. His wife, Sabina, was also arrested and sentenced to hard labor, leaving their son homeless and alone.

After he was released, Wurmbrand returned to his evangelistic work. He was rearrested and sentenced to twenty-five years for undermining the Communist doctrine. In 1965, a Norwegian church ransomed him for ten thousand dollars. He was released and eventually ended up in America where he stood before a U.S. Senate Security Internal Subcommittee, where he stripped off his shirt to reveal the deep scars from his torture. His testimony shocked everyone.

He chronicled that testimony in *Tortured for Christ*[7], a book that continues to be widely read. Through his ministry, Voice of the Martyrs, information on the treatment of Christians under Communism spread through the Western world. His prayer for the Romanian underground church was one of the reasons Brother Andrew and Open Doors sought the right couriers for the Bible smuggling mission.

Brother Andrew was right to send us because we were Americans. At the time, Ceausescu was seen as a maverick by the Soviet Union and was being courted by the West. Since no free news agencies existed in Romania, the plight of the people was not really known.

Our mission was simple. We were to drive to Bucharest, the capital city, make contact with Dr. Constantinescu, deliver the Bibles and return. The trip would take a little over a week—a piece of cake. We would travel in a Ford diesel camper van that would transport five thousand Bibles, twenty-five hundred songbooks, and two containers of precious printer's ink. Printer's ink was banned in Romania because it could be used to print seditious material. We were told that on the Black Market, our contraband would fetch close to a million dollars.

It wasn't until many years after our mission that a great deal of information became available about what had been going on in Romania under President Ceausescu. During his regime, he instituted a brutal program of systematization, which called for the demolition of more than thirteen thousand villages, including many ancient Hungarian and German settlements.

When a major earthquake hit Bucharest in March of 1977, a few months before we arrived, whole areas of the city were destroyed. This began Ceausescu's megalomaniacal vision of *systematization*, a nationwide program to remove hundreds of small villages, many of them centuries old, that were deemed economically inefficient. This program had a devastating effect on the citizens. People lost their homes, their livelihood, and their hope. Farms were co-opted to become "the People's Farms." Many were forced to work in the mines or move to the cities. Poverty was rampant.

When we arrived in June, Ceausescu was concentrating on Bucharest. Although we didn't know it at the time, over one-fifth of the city, including churches and historical buildings, were demolished in order to rebuild the city as a symbol of "a multilaterally developed socialist republic." When we were in Bucharest, we saw the devastation but thought it was all earthquake-related.

To accomplish his plan of rapid industrialization, the Romanian president relied heavily on foreign money, which mired his country in debt and resulted in an economic disaster. Food rationing was introduced and the average Romanian citizen had to fight for survival.

Long queues for toilet paper, bread, and meat were the norms. Heating, gas, and electricity blackouts became the rule. The country was in turmoil. Tensions were mounting, not only because of Ceausescu's policies but also because of the growing power of the secret police.

Ceausescu's secret police, the *Securitate*, was one of the largest and most brutal forces in existence in the Eastern Bloc. Any opposition was crushed. According to some sources, the Securitate employed some 11,000 agents and more than 500,000 informers. They would be our biggest threat. No more than four people were allowed to gather at the same time (not in the streets or at home), except in the government-sanctioned churches where Ceausescu's Communist manifesto was intoned, or at schools and universities.

As an avowed atheist, Ceausescu consigned thousands of Christians to mental institutions where inhumane experiments were conducted. Open Doors was determined to help the Romanian underground church in its time of need.

Ceausescu's insane program to reform his country and its people by force was carried out behind the Iron Curtain. The West was allowed to see only what Ceausescu wanted seen. He made several visits to America and England, promising cooperation in exchange for foreign aid.

Washington salivated at the chance of having an "ally" within the Soviet Bloc. Ceausescu knew this and, being the con man that he was, played his hand well and received money from the West, which he used to continue his crazy social reform and to build a palace as extravagant as anything in Europe.[8]

Anecdotally, there was a rumor circulating that when the Ceausescus came to visit the West (England and America), all the valuables were removed from the rooms and/or replaced with cheap copies because the couple had a reputation for stealing anything that wasn't nailed down, including lamps, rugs, and wall and bathroom fixtures.

It wasn't until after the revolution in 1989 that the United States, England, and most European countries renounced him and rescinded any honors they had bestowed on him. But at the time of our mission, Ceausescu was courting the West, desperate for American money to shore up his dwindling treasury, and he would welcome American tourists into his country.

# CHAPTER 5

# On Our Way

On a sunny June day, representatives of Open Doors came to the Shalom House and delivered to us a beautiful, blue Ford diesel camper van. No one would ever guess it was an artfully equipped smuggler's van.

The children were already settled with our friends. It had been hard to say goodbye to them, but they didn't seem to understand what a week was, so I prayed that the time would go quickly for them and that they would not be anxious or sad. After accepting the mission, this had been one of the most difficult decisions we had to make. We prayed about it and decided it was best to leave the children behind. We asked them whom they would like to stay with and they chose a couple from our church who readily agreed to the arrangement.

For over a week we would have no communication with them. I was not worried that it would traumatize them. The boys were extremely resilient and very secure. Still, it would be hard to leave them behind, not knowing what awaited us. I believed, as did my husband, that we would not encounter any trouble. We were filled with faith about this trip.

I was convinced that God had us in the palm of His hand. Fear never lingered long in my mind. I was able to convey this to the children and told them I would be bringing them back some gifts from Romania.

When the camper van pulled up with an Open Doors volunteer driving another car behind it, all our immediate "family" from the Shalom House came outside to look at the special van. My husband received many slaps on the back, and I received many hugs. Friends encircled us, held hands, and began to pray over us. I couldn't hold back the tears.

As excited as everyone was, there was a somber mood pervading the conversations. They all knew what we were facing, but were also filled with faith and gave us words of encouragement. I knew these brothers and sisters in Christ would be interceding for us the entire time.

The men from Open Doors went over all the fine points of smuggling. We listened carefully to everything they said. They showed us the secret unlocking mechanism that would release the side and floor panels, which would reveal the Bibles and songbooks, translated into the Romanian language. Looking inside the van, it was hard to believe that there were five thousand Romanian Bibles, twenty-five hundred songbooks and bottles of printer's ink hidden in the walls and under the floor of the van.

The most dangerous part of the journey would be when we unlocked the panels and brought the Bibles out into the open. We had no idea how we were going to do this, but this trip was all about trusting God to lead the way and protect us on our mission.

The van contained a refrigerator, a two-burner propane stove, and a sink. There was a bench on either side and they showed us how to fold out the platform and move the cushions to make a double bed.

The bench on the passenger side was shorter than the other because next to it was a table top on hinges, placed flat against the wall (this would be removed when we opened the side panels, as would the benches). Under the benches were storage compartments where we could put our clothes, toiletries and canned goods. It was a very compact space.

Before they left, the Open Doors representatives gave us a map detailing our route to the border of Romania. Beyond that, there was no map to lead us. No current map of Romania's interior was known to exist. They suggested that we go north toward Transylvania and look for signs to Bucharest that would take us due south. They suggested that there was bound to be a direct route out of the north from Hungary to Bucharest, the capital of Romania. They believed this but didn't know for sure.

They gave us the address and apartment number where our contact lived in Bucharest. Then they gave us the names and addresses of two alternate contacts in case we were unable to make contact with the first. From their instructions, we wrote these addresses on pieces of gum, rewrapped them in the silver paper and slipped them back into the sleeve. I returned the gum to the pack and put it in the glove box.

They also cautioned us to be careful not to be recognized as Americans. When in public, we were to speak to each other only if no one could hear our English. They had us memorize the number of the tram we were to use to get to our contact and the exact change to use so we wouldn't have to ask and reveal that we were foreigners. It gave me a chill. It was so cloak and dagger.

Before we crossed the border, we were to destroy the contact information. It would be up to us, once in Bucharest, to find a map that would lead us there. They asked us to collect as many maps as we could in Yugoslavia and Romania since it would make future missions easier. Yes, we were like pilgrims crossing the Atlantic. We did not know what we would face—danger was assured—but our faith would lead us on.

Since we didn't have a map of the country, we would have to follow road signs. We were to travel from the Netherlands through Germany and into Austria. It was there we would cross the border into the Socialist Republic of Yugoslavia. President Josip Broz Tito had relaxed travel restrictions for foreigners, but this crossing would still be dangerous. If our contraband was discovered, we could be jailed for smuggling. I did not want to see the inside of a Yugoslavian jail.

The real danger would be crossing the border into Romania. Our every move would be scrutinized. We were told that we were required to report our daily activities to the park officials, including any conversations with Romanian citizens.

We didn't sleep well that night. We were up early, packed our things into the van and loaded the refrigerator with food. We left Leusden around seven in the morning and drove south for an hour to Arnhem, Holland. Another thirty minutes and we were at the German border.

"*Guten tag,*" I said to the border guard. He nodded his head and took our passports. He went into the booth and returned shortly. He handed them to us. I looked at the visa stamp on the page.

"God bless you and your family," I said in German.

He smiled and said, "*Danke.*"

"That's one down," Lon said, as he put the van in gear and we drove into Germany.

"Three to go," I replied.

We made good time on the autobahn. There wasn't a speed limit on the German highway, so we stayed in the middle or far right lane. Woe to any who got in the way of the high-performance cars in the far left lane. They traveled at supersonic speeds compared to our camper van.

As a silver Porsche whizzed by us, Lon joked, "If you see it in your rearview, it has already passed you."

"They're crazy," I said as a Mercedes-Benz zoomed by.

"If we weren't carrying a load of Bibles, I'd show them what this little baby can do." He tapped the dashboard.

"When we come back, you'll have your chance."

He looked at me. "Yeah. When we come back."

We played music, sang, talked, and enjoyed the beautiful scenery. We'd been on this road many times before and it felt like we were on vacation. We stopped at a camping ground outside Köln and had breakfast at a picnic table. We greeted people as they walked by. The camper was stocked with canned foods and refrigerated items, so we had cold cereal and bread with honey.

After breakfast, we walked around awhile. We would have a long drive to the Austrian border, so we soaked up the sun and fresh air.

I struck up a conversation with a young German couple and stumbled through my limited German vocabulary. I learned that they were on vacation and heading toward Holland's capital city, The Hague. I told them what I could before we erupted into laughter as the language failed me. As we walked back to the van, my husband asked me what they had said.

"They probably spoke English, why'd you insist on German? I hate to tell you, but you're a little rusty."

"I know. I'm terrible at it. I just felt like I needed the practice."

"They don't speak German in Romania, honey."

"Well, you never know. It might come in handy."

We got back on the autobahn and drove another three hours to Nürenburg. We took a break for lunch at a rest stop outside the city. I heated up some soup and made sandwiches.

"Can you believe we're doing this?" he asked, munching on his sandwich. We had the door open and sat at the table inside the van. It was hot and there wasn't even a breeze to cool us off.

"No. I don't think it ever entered my mind. Following Jesus has been an adventure, hasn't it?"

"Well, I know we wouldn't be living in Holland if it wasn't for Him. I'd be in Thailand," he said as he wiped his arm across his sweating forehead.

"And I'd be raising the kids alone in the California desert. God has been good to us. He has always met our needs," I said, pulling a blond strand of hair away from my face.

"Remember when we first got married, living in the Oregon mountains, how poor we were; how we had to live by faith?" he said, smiling at the recollection.

I nodded. The memory was poignant. "We didn't even have money for groceries. Remember? I'll never forget that time when we were out of money and had no food in the house. All we had was a half head of lettuce, an onion, and a nearly empty jar of peanut butter. I prayed and then ransacked the cupboards. There was nothing there. I got down on my knees and prayed for help. I looked again, reached way back into the cupboard and my hand felt something—a package of spaghetti noodles and a can of tomato soup."

I laughed, remembering how I had turned that can of soup into a marinara sauce.

Lon grinned. "I remember. Oh boy, do I remember. We ate spaghetti for a week. As grateful as I was, I was sick of it by the end."

"I know. Right? Who knew it would last so long. It was to feed us that night, but there was enough left over for the next night, and the next, and the next. Every time I pulled it out of the fridge, it was the same amount as the first night. It just never seemed to go down."

"The amazing proliferating spaghetti!"

I laughed and said, "And when you got your paycheck and we could go grocery shopping, I actually had to throw out leftovers!"

"That was an honest to God miracle, wasn't it?" he said, touching my hand.

I placed my hand over his. "Yes. God was watching over us then and is watching over us now."

"Finish up. We should get going. I want to make the Austrian border before nightfall."

I rinsed the soup pan, tidied the kitchen area, and filled our water jug. We got back onto the autobahn and headed south. We passed Koblenz, Stuttgart, and München. It was around seven in the evening when we crossed our second border into Austria. We had been on the road for twelve hours.

The border guard was very kind. He gave us a map and showed us where we could camp outside Salzburg, one of my favorite European cities.

"Two to go," we said at the same time and laughed.

We found the campground, paid our fee, and then drove into Salzburg for an evening meal. We found a quaint little restaurant and ate a modest meal of potatoes, sausage, and applesauce. We strolled down the beautiful streets of Mozart's birthplace, looking into shop windows and admiring the architecture.

We returned to the campground, set up our bed, and waited for sleep. Even though it had been a long day of driving, we couldn't settle down. We would be driving into Yugoslavia by late morning. It was difficult to sleep because our excitement had turned to nervous anticipation. It would be our first big test of faith.

We woke refreshed. In honor of our upcoming border crossing, I fixed bacon and eggs and brewed a pot of coffee. The air was crisp and chilly. There wasn't a cloud in the sky.

Preparing for the long ride ahead, we took a brisk walk and stretched our legs. The air was fragrant with the smell of wildflowers. The majestic Alps surrounded us, making us feel small. We were thankful that we were not attempting this trip in the winter. The land shadowed by the purple mountains was comprised of various shades of green with brilliant white snow capping the tips of the jagged peaks.

From Salzburg, we traveled south toward the Yugoslavian border (which is now Slovenia). We followed the Alps. The mountains rose from the valley floor like a giant comb of granite. Nothing compares to the sudden thrust of these mountains, blue against a green sea of lush vegetation, but Hohe Tauern National Park reminded me of Teton National Park in Wyoming.

As we left this park behind we drove into the Nockberge National Park, the oldest mountain range in Austria. Unlike the Hohe Tauern with its majestic beauty, the landscape was one of gently rolling mountains and hilltops.

We were traveling at a steady speed but had to stop suddenly because a flock of fleecy white sheep flooded the road. We watched in silence as the massive herd poured down from the mountainside like a waterfall.

"Look over there," Lon said, pointing to one lone sheep that had become separated from the flock. It was standing on a rocky ledge, terrified and bleating.

"Oops, someone's gone the wrong direction," I said, laughing.

"He zigged when he should have zagged."

"I don't see the shepherd. How do these sheep know to cross the road here?"

We scanned the mountainside looking for a human. The sheep were all around the van at this point, wandering en masse to the other side of the road and down into a ravine of crisp green grass where they stopped to eat.

"There," Lon shouted, pointing upward.

We watched as a man appeared from the opposite side of the slope, angling his descent to coincide with the wayward sheep. He made steady progress down the treacherous hillside until he finally reached the lone sheep.

We saw him examine the animal's legs, then in one swift motion, he grabbed the legs and slung it over his head to rest on his neck. He carried the sheep all the way down the mountain until he reached level ground. He let it go. It scampered after its companions.

"You know what that reminds me of?" Lon asked, staring out the window.

"Uh-huh," I said. "We've just seen a parable in action."

"He could have left it," he said. "After all, it was just one dumb sheep and he has thousands. He'd never miss it."

"For whatever reason," I said, my heart beating hard from the poignancy of what we had seen, "it was more important to risk his life for that one sheep than herd the others that seemed to know where they were going."

Right at that time, three men, a boy, and a dog appeared on the neighboring slope and began shooing the rest of the sheep down the mountain. The flock trotted across the valley floor and took over the road in front of us.

Following along, the shepherds clucked their tongues, shouted, and used a rod to tap the behinds of the sheep, causing them to scamper off the road so that we had room to pass. We didn't mind waiting because we were in a state of wonder.

The shepherd who had rescued the one sheep lifted his arm and waved to us, indicating that we could move on. We complied and waved to him as we passed. Now there was nothing to hinder us. We were on our way to the Yugoslavian border with a deep assurance that our Good Shepherd was watching over us.

# CHAPTER 6

# Can You Say Map?

We had been on the road three hours, one of which had been spent sitting in the van watching the sheep. It gave us time to determine our route into Yugoslavia. After much consideration, we decided to risk the Wurzenpaß, a road through the Alps with an elevation of 1073 meters or 3520 feet.

We believed that by entering Yugoslavia from this rather remote border crossing, it would make us less vulnerable to a search. If we had known that the road would go straight up, without any switchbacks, I don't think we would have taken it. As we drove up the pass, the diesel engine chugged along steadily, but we had to drive nearly all the way in first gear.

The scenery was spectacular. On one side of the narrow two-lane road was a dense coniferous forest. The air was crisp and fragrant, smelling of pine. On my side of the road was a sheer cliff. I could smell the clutch smoking as we inched up the incline. It reminded me of when I was a child and my father accidentally drove onto a forest service road in the Rocky Mountains, pulling our trailer. My brothers were in the back seat at the ready with large rocks to wedge under the wheels of the trailer if we had to stop. I almost wanted to get out of the camper van and get a big rock, just in case.

Several trucks were pulled over on the side of the road, their radiators spewing steam, their drivers wiping their brows in frustration. We passed them, praying we would not share the same fate. What would happen if our vehicle overheated and we were stranded so close to the border in our specially equipped smuggling van? We had to trust God to get us to the top.

We were relieved and anxious when we saw the border crossing at the top of the pass. We knew we had arrived at the Yugoslavian border. There was a stark white building on the left side, with a red and white crossing bar lowered across the road. The place looked deserted, but as we slowed to a stop in front of the crossing bar, two soldiers with rifles slung over their shoulders stepped out to meet us.

One soldier came to the driver's side. Lon rolled down the window and gave him a big American smile. The guard did not smile back. He wore an olive green uniform with a cap on his head. His rifle hung casually over his shoulder, but its presence made us realize that this was our first serious test.

We handed over our passports. He was surprised to see that we were Americans. He showed them to his companion and they began an animated conversation that we couldn't understand. They indicated that Lon was to get out of the van. They opened the door and he got out. I began to pray even harder.

They asked him questions, but he couldn't understand them. He just smiled. I smiled. We looked like a couple of naive young sightseers—obviously rich Americans, given the newness of our van. Their curiosity became more intense.

Two more soldiers came out of the guard shack and asked what was going on. They passed our passports around, exclaiming and looking us over carefully. Obviously, they didn't have too many travelers come this way, and after the long trek up the mountain, I could see why.

Two of the soldiers followed their curiosity and indicated they wanted my husband to open the back of the van. My heart leaped in my throat. I began to pray intensely, as Lon reluctantly opened the back doors for them.

While two soldiers led Lon back to the building, the other two stepped into the van and sat on the padded benches that served as our bed. They patted the cushions. They were talking to each other and I could tell they were impressed with the economical simplicity of our camper van. From the front passenger seat, I kept my eyes on them as Lon did what he was supposed to do. He asked the other two soldiers for a map.

"Map," he said. "Do you have a map? You know, map."

I could see him pantomiming, driving a car and outlining a big square. The guards were thoroughly confused. They stepped in closer, trying to figure out what Lon was doing.

While Lon tried to get a map from the soldiers at the guard shack, the soldiers in the back of the van were admiring the amenities of our little camper. Suddenly, one of the soldiers became curious about a particular area of the van. He pointed it out to his companion. He got up and began examining it. My stomach did a flip-flop. I didn't know what to do! The unlocking mechanism was nearby. If he continued his search he was sure to discover it.

There was an opening between the driver and passenger's seats, so when we were driving, I was able to get up and fix snacks or get drinks when needed. I jumped out of my seat, not knowing what I was going to do, and stepped into the back to interrupt the search.

Just then, the soldiers outside erupted in laughter. I glanced across to where Lon was speaking to them, trying to explain what he wanted. He was still pantomiming, but now the guards were thoroughly engaged in guessing what he was trying to say. The two guards outside laughed and slapped him on the back; as if they thought he was having some kind of fit. He tried harder, which made them laugh even more, trying to figure out what this crazy American was trying to say.

The soldiers inside heard their comrades laughing and looked out the side windows to find out what was going on. The soldier who was examining the interior of the van stopped his search just shy of the latch that would open the side panels. He turned and joined his companion who was already stepping out of the back of the van. They shut the doors and joined the growing hilarity. I breathed a sigh of relief—but not for long.

When I got back to my seat, I looked out the window. There was my husband surrounded by four armed soldiers. He was saying over and over, "Map, you know, map (he drew a square with his fingers), so we can get around the streets (at this he swam his hand around like he was weaving down a road)." They shook their heads, laughing, and handed him our passports. He opened the driver side door and got in behind the wheel. He looked at me and grinned.

"I guess they don't understand English," he said. "I wasn't able to get us a map."

The red and white cross bar rose up in front of us. The four soldiers saluted as we drove forward. We waved to them and they waved back, big grins on their faces. Lon drove immediately into the parking lot of the bank at the border and parked. We needed to change our money into Yugoslavian currency. The trip across Yugoslavia would be long.

"One of the guards started looking at the unlocking mechanism," I whispered. "If you hadn't made them laugh…"

"We're okay," he said, grabbing my hand. "God is with us. Look. We're in Yugoslavia."

We had not only entertained the border guards, we had crossed into Yugoslavia.

"Praise God! One to go!" we shouted.

# CHAPTER 7

## Yugoslavian Sunflowers

The view was breathtaking as we descended the mountain. Tall pines rose skyward on either side, reaching up to downy white clouds that glided across a cobalt sky. The verdant valley below was dotted with red-roofed farmhouses and grey-shingled barns. There didn't appear to be any difference between the landscape in Austria and Yugoslavia.

From what we knew about Yugoslavia, even though it was a Communist country, its citizens enjoyed greater freedom than any of the other Eastern Bloc countries. We had no trouble changing our money at the bank and the clerk was very friendly. It didn't feel like a rigid Communist country.

What we didn't know is that prior to our arrival, growing unrest among the different nationalities in Yugoslavia had increased, primarily among the Croats and Serbians. President Tito had restricted the actions of intellectuals to keep nationalistic tendencies under wraps, but despite his controls, the six republics and the autonomous province of Serbia were beginning to flex their nationalistic muscles. It would only be a matter of time before civil war broke out.

As we drove around a sharp curve in the road, our eyes fixed on the scenery, Lon braked in time to avoid plowing into a slow-moving wooden cart. Everything shifted in the back of the van and my water spilled all over my lap. One of the four cows tethered to the back of the cart turned his head and mooed, as if to say, "Watch it, buddy!"

Two huge oxen pulled the cart. Heavy wooden yokes strapped them together. A man, who held the reins, walked slowly beside them, completely unaware of how close he had come to being rear-ended by our van. Tied to the cart were four cows who were aware of the close call. One turned its head and mooed a warning.

"We thought crossing a Communist border was dangerous; but nobody told us we'd nearly kill ourselves on the road," Lon said, wiping his sweaty hands on his lap. "There's no way I can go around them. The road's too narrow and with all the twists and turns, I don't dare try to pass them."

"Only one car's passed us so far," I replied.

"You want to risk it?"

I looked beyond the cart, but the bend in the road impeded my view. It was a very narrow road. We would have to pass on the cliff's edge and there were no guardrails. I shivered at the thought.

"We can't afford to get into an accident. I guess we'll just have to assume the pace of an ox," I said, laughing.

"Okay, now. What's that scripture about yokes?" Lon asked.

"You mean, 'take my yoke upon you, and learn of me; for I am meek and lowly in heart: and ye shall find rest for your souls...'"

"For my yoke is easy, and my burden is light," he finished.

"Another scripture in action," I said. "Do you think God is purposefully showing us these things or is it just a coincidence?"

"Does it matter?" he said. "The main thing is that these moments remind us of His Word. If you weren't a Christian transporting five thousand Bibles, maybe you'd think it was a coincidence."

"And we'd probably be cursing our heads off because of the delay."

"Instead, we can thank God for showing us He is with us."

Lon rolled down his window. I followed suit. We began to sing at the top of our voices.

"Praise God from whom all blessings flow. Praise Him all creatures here below. Praise Him above, ye heavenly hosts. Praise Father, Son and Holy Ghost."

The air was tangy, sweet, and cool. We adjusted our pace to the leisurely walk of a cow, a man, and a cart, and took the moment to really look at the scenery as our songs of praise filled the van. Every once in awhile, the vocal cow would lend his voice to ours and punctuate our lyrics.

"The joy of the Lord is my strength."

"Moo!"

"The joy of the Lord is my strength."

"Moo!"

As we took another hairpin curve on the road, we saw that ahead of the cart was another car crawling along. Ahead of that car was a large brown tarp-covered truck. As the road curved out to the left, we saw why the car and truck were driving so slowly.

A convoy of military vehicles, including a tank, was winding its way down the sharp decline of the mountain pass. If we had passed the oxen and cart, we would have run straight into the Yugoslavian military. We just looked at each other. No words were needed.

Eventually, the convoy pulled off onto a dirt road at the bottom of the mountain. We easily passed the oxen and cart and waved to the man holding the reins. He just stared at us.

The landscape changed dramatically. The steep, forested mountains gave way to farmland. To the west was the bustling village of Podkoren and to the east were acres and acres of alfalfa fields. These were interspersed with rows of towering trees that served as windbreaks. We traveled on the valley floor between the southern range of the Julian Alps. These magnificent mountains loomed above us on either side, casting deep shadows across the road.

The sloping mountains gave way to rolling hills of deep green forests. Our small, narrow road ended and we turned onto a major highway towards Zagreb. The road was well paved and we made time. The snow-capped Alps receded to the horizon.

Our route paralleled the Sava River, a large tributary of the famous Danube. We passed many small towns that flourished near the river, which flowed all the way to Belgrade where it emptied into the Danube.

Lush farmland once again took over the landscape, interspersed with dense forests. The trees nearly blotted out the sun as we continued to travel south. As we left the forest behind, square, boxy houses, with characteristic red-orange roofs came into view. The towns became closer together and grew in population as we came to the city of Ljubljana.

This city was among the most beautiful I had ever seen. Driving through it, we were struck by its Baroque architecture and how much it reminded us of Salzburg—castle included.

In 1991, after the civil war, Yugoslavia was dissolved and Ljubljana would become the capital of Slovenia, which entered the European Union in 2004. The Ljubljanica River, which is also called the River of Seven Names, flows straight through the city. Many beautiful bridges spanned the river, reminding me of Venice.

The first bridge we crossed was reputed to have been built by the Romans. With the Alps looming in the background and the tree-lined embankments of the river, Ljubljana was a popular tourist stop. If we had had the time, I would have loved to spend a few days there. But we were on a mission.

We reluctantly left Ljubljana and turned southeast toward Zagreb. Onion-shaped domes of Eastern Orthodox churches could be seen in the distance. We always knew where a village was when we saw those distinctive silhouettes. At this time, the church was under strict control by the state and the teaching of religion in schools was prohibited. In the Communist state, people were discouraged from religious activity. Many of these beautiful churches had been taken over by the state and used for other purposes.

As we passed numerous small farming villages, we took to counting stork nests in the chimneys of the houses we passed. These were big birds, about forty to fifty inches high with a wingspan of more than sixty inches. The stork is a white bird with black wings, a red beak, and red legs. To have a stork nest in your chimney was considered good luck, but it didn't appear to be working. The wooden houses were often dilapidated.

We left the Alps behind and entered the grassy plain of the Sava River valley. It took us less than two hours to arrive in Zagreb, even with the sudden lengthy stops. These were sometimes due to roadwork, sometimes to let various animals cross the road, or to allow slow-moving carts to pull to the side. Even then, in 1977 Zagreb, now the capital of Croatia, was a large city with a population of over 600,000.

The city lies between the southern slopes of the Medvednica Mountains and the northern and southern banks of the Sava River. It was established in 1092 and retained some of its medieval charms, but to our eyes, the city looked very industrial and drab.

Modern high-rise buildings and a bustling commercial district contrasted with crumbling old buildings and the rising spires of a huge Gothic cathedral. During the Croatian War of Independence in the nineties, Zagreb would be spared and most of its buildings would remain intact.

After a quick bite to eat in the van, we were off to Belgrade, the capital. It took about four more hours to get there. One of the oldest cities in Europe (as far back as the sixth millennium BC), it has one of the most significant prehistoric Neolithic settlements in Eastern Europe. Most likely this is because Belgrade sits at the confluence of two great rivers, the Sava and the Danube, and is where the Pannonian Plain meets the Balkan Peninsula. In 2000, after a brutal war, the citizens of Belgrade ousted the Serbian President Slobodan Milosevic, who was later tried as a war criminal after the Yugoslav Wars. The city is now the capital of Serbia.

When we came into Belgrade, we looked for a campground for the night. With all the stops along the way due to the rural nature of the area, we had been on the road for more than ten hours. It didn't take long to find a campground. It was clearly marked but it was not what we expected.

The campground was more like a motel, but we were allowed to park in the parking lot for one hundred *dinars*, about a dollar-fifty. We parked the van and got ready for bed. We were so tired we didn't even talk. We just rolled onto the cushions and fell into a dreamless sleep.

We awoke to the sounds of traffic. We decided to take some time to sightsee. Our legs were cramped and we thought a brisk stroll would do us good. This would be our last stop in Yugoslavia before crossing the border into Romania.

One of the most dramatic places we visited was St. Mark's Church. We also viewed the Parliament Building, a beautiful domed, granite edifice. After walking around the city, we found a small outdoor cafe and stopped for coffee and conversation.

"So, let's talk about our plan," Lon said softly. "Once we get to Bucharest, we'll have to find a campground or some place where we can park without drawing suspicion."

"I'm sure we'll find one," I replied. "The Black Sea is popular with the Eastern tourists and they'll have to drive through Bucharest to get there."

"Let's pray that's the case," Lon nodded and then clamped his mouth shut as the waiter walked by. We watched him as he cleared a table near us. He never once looked our way, so Lon resumed our conversation. "So once we camp, I figure we'll need at least one whole day to act like tourists. We'll want to see the sights."

"I hope we don't stick out too much. Do you think we look like Americans?"

"We'll do what Brother Andrew did and pray that the Lord makes seeing eyes blind. There's nothing we can do about being Americans. From what he says, Americans have a tendency to strut. We'll have to slump our shoulders more."

"You're making that up," I laughed.

"I'm serious. Brother Andrew said that Americans carry a presence of independence and freedom about them. We've never been oppressed, so we stick out."

"Let's pray that never changes," I said, contemplating his words. I had never thought about it. Did we have a freedom strut?

We sipped on our coffee and watched the passersby. I scrutinized the way the women dressed, and I'm sure Lon was doing the same with the men. Their clothes lacked color, but otherwise they were your standard European suit, dress, slacks, blouse, and shirt.

"The next day, we'll make contact," Lon continued. "Then they'll take it from there."

"What if we can't get a map? How will we find the address," I asked.

"That's up to God," he reminded me. "If we can't find a map, we'll just wander around and let the Spirit lead us."

I looked up sharply, eyeing him for signs of instability. He was grinning at me.

"Don't mock the Lord, Lon. We may have to do just that." He stopped grinning and gave my hand a squeeze.

"We'll be okay, honey," he said. "So what if we stick out. There's no law against being an American tourist."

"That we know of," I said soberly.

"What's wrong?"

"I'm sorry," I said, noting his concern. "I'm just thinking about how we'll look when we go into the residential areas. It's one thing to be a tourist in the designated tourist spots, but once we head into the neighborhoods, we can't afford to look like we don't belong there."

"I know you're worried, honey," he said, trying to reassure me, "but if God isn't with us on this, we were doomed before we left Holland. We made it across this border, didn't we?"

"We did. I will never forget how I felt when all those soldiers were surrounding you. I thought we were going to be arrested, and then they all burst out laughing. You did look pretty comical."

"I never had to do charades for a map before." He demonstrated his attempt again. We laughed and the mood lightened.

I shrugged my shoulders. "Beyond that, I guess we don't know what will happen, do we?"

"No, we don't," he said. "We have to trust the Lord for every step we take from now on."

"I'm ready," I said, giving him my bravest face.

"Me, too. Let's pay the bill and get on the road. If God be for us, who can be against us!"

"Only about a million informers and secret police."

"Piece of cake," he said, laying down five *dinars*. "Our God is bigger than that."

We got up and walked back to the van.

We left the city and traveled on Route E70 through miles of flat fields of wheat, corn, alfalfa, clover, and sunflowers. The scenery was monotonous, but every once in awhile was sprinkled with small villages and farms.

We began admiring the different ways the farmers dried their straw and hay, some folded over on tall wooden racks, some compacted into large rolls, some stacked in standard hay bales, some piled into immense mounds, and some slanted together as vertical sheaths. From the road, some looked like great yellow cities in the distance.

At one point we had to slow to a crawl behind a horse-drawn cart filled with straw. The mound was three times the size of the cart and a boy sat precariously on top, with stray pieces of yellow straw filling the air like showers of gold.

There was no way to pass them on the tiny two-lane road. As with the oxen on the mountain pass, we just had to be patient. I rolled down the window and tried to catch straw floating in the air. At last, the cart turned off onto a dirt road. I watched with my heart in my throat as the boy balanced on the slippery straw that bounced and jostled through the turn, leaving a trail of yellow.

We soon came upon a field of sunflowers. After the lack of color we had found in the cities and villages, the waving stalks of sunflowers were a welcome sight. We passed miles and miles of the pretty yellow flowers. Earlier during my initial research, I had learned that sunflower seeds were harvested, processed into oil and exported to other Eastern Bloc countries. I found it a bit ironic that Native Americans were the first to cultivate the sunflower. It was the Spanish explorers of America that brought the plant to the European continent, where it flourishes today.

Yugoslavia proved to be the perfect climate for this beautiful plant. Our last glimpse of the country before we reached the Romanian border fifteen miles ahead was a vast sea of sunflowers, stretching miles in all directions. It gladdened my heart to see their lovely heads waving in the breeze.

As we proceeded to the border, I thought of Luke 12:27: "Consider how the wild flowers grow. They do not labor or spin. Yet I tell you, not even Solomon in all his splendor was dressed like one of these."

# CHAPTER 8

# Romania

As we neared the Romanian border, my husband pulled off the road under a large, leafy tree. We went into the back of the van to collect our thoughts, review our plans, and pray.

"How're you feeling?" he asked.

"Nervous, scared, excited. You?"

"I'd be lying if I said I wasn't."

"It's funny," I added. "I really have peace about this. It's as if I'm covered in a big blanket of love. I have never felt His presence so close, so real. Know what I mean?"

"I do," he said, taking my hand. "It's like my brain is making lists of things to be worried about, but they don't stick. I just feel—I don't know—like it's not me doing this."

"I know what you mean. I've felt it since we began. Like God wants this more than we do; like we don't have anything to do with it except to be His hands and feet."

"So let's go over everything one more time."

We had been instructed to park in an official tourist campground in Bucharest. We hoped that the international sign for camping—a blue teepee or tent—would guide the way. It wasn't that unusual to have a campground in a major city.

Travel among Eastern Bloc countries was without restriction, and just as with American tourists, camping was a popular way of spending a vacation. What was not like America was that we were required to register as tourists at the campground office and report on every place we visited.

Once we were settled, we were to establish ourselves as tourists before making contact with Dr. Constantinescu. He didn't know we were coming, so we had two other backup names. Once we made contact with him, he would arrange for the transfer of our cargo. How and when we made contact were up to us. When we got over the border, our hope was that road signs would lead us to Bucharest.

Once we had reviewed everything we knew, the only thing left to do was pray. We held hands as we prayed.

"Lord, you have called us to your service, to help your persecuted church. We ask for your protection as we cross the border. Bind the devil and keep us safe. Help us make good decisions and guide us as we seek out our contact in an unknown land. We place our lives in your care. In Jesus' name, Amen."

I flipped open my Bible and pointed to a scripture. A tear fell on the page as I read Luke 12:11-12.

"When you are brought before synagogues, rulers and authorities, do not worry about how you will defend yourselves or what you will say, for the Holy Spirit will teach you at that time what you should say."

"Well, I hope that doesn't mean we're going to get caught," Lon said glumly.

"Me, too," I said, gulping. "God is with us. We must have faith and believe He will get us through."

"Okay, then, let's do this."

We scrambled into our seats. I pulled the pack of gum from the glove box and found the specific piece of gum with our contacts' information written on it. We memorized the three addresses and names and popped the gum into our mouths. Lon put the van in gear and went forward, knowing that the four other missions before us had been foiled. We could only pray that we would be successful.

As we pulled up behind a line of cars, I prayed under my breath. "Lord, be with us, protect us, lead us through this barrier."

This border crossing was nothing like the one in Yugoslavia. This one was drop-dead serious. A stark wide roof spanned from one side of the highway to the other. The building on the right was much larger and the guards were very thorough. There was an oppressive spirit about the whole area.

We watched in dismay as the cars in front of us were put through exhaustive searches. Our brand new, blue diesel Ford camper van stood out from all the worn out cars and trucks in front of us. We, as twenty-something Americans, would certainly be noticed. We knew we would be an object of curiosity just as we had been at the Yugoslavian border.

One by one the cars in front of us passed through the border after intensive searches. We were now one car away from their scrutiny. The little white car in front of us would not take long to search, even though it was piled high with bundles on its roof. I could see by its license plate that it was from Morocco—a long way from home, but then so were we. The little white car pulled up to the border crossing.

Four machine-gun armed guards approached the car. They opened both the driver and passenger doors and ordered the occupants to get out. Two men got out and were instructed to sit on the curb.

From my vantage point, I could see that they were scared. They were in their late twenties, dark-haired, olive-skinned, wearing white shirts and black pants. One had a long moustache; the other was clean-shaven. They spoke to each other until one of the guards came over and yelled at them, making them hang their heads and stop talking.

The border guards examined every square inch of the vehicle. They took all the bundles off the top of the car and tore them open, scattering the contents all over the pavement. They looked under the hood and in the trunk. They pulled out the suitcases and bags inside the car and set them aside.

We watched in growing anxiety as they pulled the front seats and then the back seat out of the car. They seemed to be very intent on what lay beneath the seats.

One guard got down onto the road and looked under the car. Another opened the suitcases and bags, dumping the clothes onto the road. The suitcases were then torn apart. The floor mats were pulled out. Everything from the trunk was pulled out. We couldn't believe it when two of the guards began to rip apart the seats. They were convinced something was there.

Even after witnessing the destruction of the seats, we were unprepared for what happened next. The guards unhinged and removed both doors from the car. They ripped out the side panels and abandoned them.

From my vantage point, I could see the guards were angry, frustrated and hot. Sweat poured down their faces. Dark circles grew under their arms. They met together and conferred. The two Moroccans were hanging on to each other.

One of the guards left the group and returned shortly with a jack. We watched in amazement as they jacked up the car, removed the tires, splitting them and finding nothing.

Now the little white car was sitting in front of us without tires, completely dismantled. It was then I noticed for the first time the sounds of insistent car horns behind us.

"The line's grown quite a bit in the last two hours," Lon said, looking in the rear view mirror.

"We can't move until they move that car," I said.

"Yeah, it's going to be a while longer. How are you doing?"

"Scared." My heart was beating fast.

"Yeah, me, too. If they do to us what they're doing to that car…"

"Let's pray!"

We grabbed onto each other's arms and prayed under our breath as we watched the guards deal with the situation they had created. In their zeal to find the contraband they were so sure was in the car, they hadn't considered the impact on regular commerce flowing across the border. Truck drivers, party officials, businessmen, tourists, and citizens were growing increasingly impatient with the delay.

I could see one of the guards talking on the telephone in the office. He was waving his arm, explaining the situation. He came out and talked with his fellow guards. Two guards came over and grabbed the Moroccans and led them into the guardhouse.

Because they had ruined the tires, they were unable to drive the vehicle out of the way. We watched incredulously as they gathered all the guards together to push the frame of the white car to one side. With their rifles slung over their shoulders, they pressed their shoulders against the car frame and pushed. The screech of metal on the hot pavement must have echoed down the line of waiting cars.

By this time, the sun was at its zenith and everyone was sweating profusely, but no one more than the guards who were dressed in olive green wool uniforms.

Once the car was pushed to the side, they waved us to go around it without a second glance. They didn't even stop us to look at our passports. We didn't dare stop and get a visa stamp. Before we knew it, we were through and had crossed into Romania miraculously unscathed.

We didn't say anything for quite a while as we drove down the narrow two-lane highway into Romania. The countryside was vast; fields on either side of the road as far as the eye could see. There were only a few clouds in the bright blue sky. The sun shone through the windows of the van, warming my arms and lap. I blinked away tears.

"Pretty country," Lon said.

"Mmm."

"I think I need to pull over."

"Okay," I murmured.

He found a dusty turnout off the road and pulled over. He shut off the engine. We looked at each other and threw ourselves into each other's arms.

"God be praised," he said after we broke apart.

"Thank you, Lord! I can't believe…"

"…They just waved us…"

"…And that poor car! Those unfortunate men! I won't forget this as long as I live," I said, wiping my eyes.

"I could barely put the van in gear, I was so…"

"Me, too."

"It just goes to show you," he said.

"The Lord goes before us," I replied.

"Amen to that. Shall we go on?"

"Onward! Christian soldier!"

We laughed and took up the song, singing at the top of our lungs. Lon pulled the van back onto the road and we headed down the two-lane road. We were on our way to the capital, Bucharest.

The task before us was daunting. We had no map to guide us. We didn't speak the language. There were secret police everywhere. No one had any idea that we were coming, bringing thousands of copies of the powerful, life-changing, liberating Word of God.

We were unstoppable.

# CHAPTER 9

# Being Tourists

From the border, the main highway was a two-lane road with tufts of grass in the cracks, particularly through the villages where traffic increased. We traveled north into Transylvania toward its capital, Cluj. From there, the main road swung south.

We were overjoyed to see the first major sign to Bucharest. We were on the right road. We had been traveling about an hour, completely without a map or the ability to ask directions; so the sight of the large highway sign that spanned the road lifted our spirits.

Many times we saw gigantic red John Deere combines working in the fields with the Soviet logo of a hammer and sickle emblazoned on the sides. Obviously, someone in America had made a deal with this country.

This agribusiness was all for export. Local farms had been co-opted and the residents had left their farms to work in the city factories.

We saw great poverty along the road—women carrying huge bundles on their heads, men herding skinny cows, undernourished children playing in the dirt near the road.

Animals crossing the road often impeded our pace, and Lon had to brake frequently to avoid hitting them. Sometimes there would be a man or boy chasing a few cows, goats or ducks off the road. Sometimes all we saw were mangy dogs barking after a few sheep and herding them into the adjacent fields. Once we had to stop for a gaggle of geese that waddled single file across the road. Their single-minded journey made us smile.

Huge factories spewed smoke out of towering smokestacks and overshadowed some of the villages we entered. We had to be very careful photographing anything in Romania because any industrialized area was considered a "government security area." If anyone reported seeing us take photos, the Securitate could pull us over and confiscate our camera.

We decided to limit taking photos while we were on the road. We risked it only one time, but the resulting photo didn't begin to convey the oppressive atmosphere that we felt as we drove past these monoliths of industry.

As we entered a village, children ran along the road and yelled, waving their hands. After the third or fourth time, we began to expect the parade of children that would greet us.

It gave us some sense of consternation that our arrival aroused such elation, but we accepted it in our role as tourists. It was possible that these children had never seen a Western European camper van such as ours. I waved back and they cheered, jumping for joy.

As we drove closer to Bucharest, we noticed the villages began to change. Before we had seen such poverty and desolation, but here we began to see beautiful mosaic buildings along the roadway. Blue, gold, and yellow ceramic tiles laid in intricate patterns covered the entire exterior of the houses. They were exquisite. I didn't expect to see these exotic houses in a country I had come to believe was poverty-stricken.

It wasn't until the large door of one of these beautiful houses opened as we passed that we caught a glimpse of what lay beyond—a dirt yard with a dilapidated wooden shack inside. We couldn't believe our eyes. Lon slowed down to a crawl as we watched in amazement as an old man led out his old, skinny cow and shut the beautiful mosaic door. It was all a facade.

We began to search for more opportunities to see what was behind the mosaic doors. Occasionally we would get another glimpse. In one dusty yard, we saw a man sitting on a stool, tending a spit above a campfire. Behind him was a straw hut with chickens pecking around the door.

Behind another mosaic wall, we saw a few children in ragged clothes kicking a can in their dusty yard. Not even Hollywood could devise such clever stagecraft to mask the poverty of an entire country. Time and time again we saw these mosaic facades and realized they were only artifices designed to project the image of a prosperous country.

Our first view of Bucharest surprised us. After miles of countryside and seeing the poverty of the people, the city looked prosperous and modern. The roads became smoother, the directions more well defined, large buildings were clustered together, and there was actual landscaping around them.

We followed the main route into the city, all the while looking for a place to camp during our short stay. As soon as we could, we found a bank. We exchanged our money for Romanian currency. The bank clerk scrutinized us, didn't understand a word we said, only that we wanted to exchange German *deutsch marks* for Romanian *leu*.

We got back into our van and drove around the city looking for campground signs. We were desperate to find a place. Suddenly, we saw a blue highway sign that showed a tent and an arrow pointing to the left. We followed the tent signs until we came to a campground within the city limits of Bucharest.

The campground was a tree-lined, grassy lawn ringed by a wire fence. We could see tents set up and small trailers parked on the edges of the lawn. We registered with the guard at the gate and paid a fee. As required, we showed him our passports. He didn't seem surprised to see American passports, but then he barely looked at them. He just wrote down the numbers on his clipboard, yawned, and gave them back to us.

We pulled our camper van into a space that was next to several small travel trailers. We could tell by the license plates on the vehicles that all were from Eastern Bloc countries. I wanted to cover our Dutch plates but at this point, it wouldn't make any difference. The hour was late by the time we were settled in. I fixed some good old-fashioned, canned American chili on our small stove. We pulled up the hinged table and inserted the pole at the end to stabilize it. We ate the chili and crackers in silence. The tension of the day had exhausted us.

From everything we knew, the Securitate was active, pervasive, and most likely had observed our arrival. The little old man at the front gate could have already reported that Americans were in the park. Every movement we made from this point on could be under their scrutiny. We wouldn't know until they picked us up, if they did. We had to trust the Lord and believe that He wanted these Bibles delivered as much as we did. We trusted that the eyes of those who would impede our mission would be blind to us.

With our dinner finished, we returned the table to its folded position, cleaned the bowls, dropped the trash in the bin outside and prepared for bed. I pulled the curtains across the windows and then adjusted the main curtain across the back of the front seats so that we were completely blocked from view.

My husband pulled out the supports that lay flat against the bench on one side. We pushed the cushion up and unfolded the bench to lie flat on the supports, and then pulled the cushion out flat to become our mattress. We put our two sleeping bags on top and crawled in. We held each other tightly as sleep finally overcame us.

We woke up the next morning to the sound of birds and the rustling of our neighbors who were preparing to leave. We got up and explored the campground, finding with relief a restroom and bathhouse. The facilities were not up to our cleanliness standards, but it had been days since we had showered. We rushed back to the van and got our toiletries and towels.

After our refreshing showers, our first order of business was to establish our cover as tourists. As much as we didn't like it, we had to play our parts for two days before making contact. We got some pamphlets from the campground guard, making a big deal of our appreciation for his help, and decided to go to the Village Museum, which was in Bucharest. It was a popular tourist destination. The museum was established in 1936 to preserve the rural life of Romania, which was rapidly changing to make way for industrialization.

As we drove to the museum, my first impression of the city was the color gray. All the brickwork, monuments, buildings, apartment complexes, everything seemed made of gray stone. A few flowering linden trees and plantings in front of government buildings were the only splashes of color we saw.

According to records from that time, approximately 35,000 buildings had been damaged or destroyed by the earthquake. Many of the historic buildings would not be restored, not only because money was unavailable, but because General Secretary Ceausescu had every intention of rebuilding Bucharest to his specifications— modern, stark and colorless. We noticed that most of the large buildings were associated with the Communist government.

The Arcul de Triumf was situated in the center of Bucharest. It was a near exact copy of the Arc de Triomphe in Paris. It was originally built of wood in 1922 to honor the soldiers of World War I, but was remade of gray granite in 1936. According to the tourist information we had, it had an interior staircase that allowed visitors to go up to the top. If we had the opportunity, we decided to make this part of our visit as tourists.

The cars that whizzed by us were all of the same make, the Dacia or Dak made by Renault. We had been told that the black Daks were for Communist Party officials. We saw many black cars.

We soon found the Village Museum and pulled into the parking lot. We walked through the entrance and were surprised to find that it was free and open to the public. At that time, it was the largest open-air museum in Europe. It was the perfect way to see the culture of Romania. Each building had been torn down and reconstructed on the museum grounds, creating a whole village.

I was very interested in the old wooden church from the Maramures. The placard outside the door indicated that it was built in the seventeenth century. Built entirely of wood, it was constructed without the use of nails. It had a narrow front porch with a wide roof.

Above this, the second story rose up to a point and from that point rose a narrow bell tower. The roof was composed of scalloped shingles that gave it a gingerbread house look. We had to duck low to enter. The ancient wooden structure was a square box that sloped upward on all sides into a peak. There was a rope across the front just inside the door so we were not able to go farther.

Inside, it was very dark, but we could see that it was filled with beautiful painted panels depicting the twelve disciples and various saints. They either had crowns on their heads or a halo. Directly across from the entrance were two arched doorways. The doors comprised full-length wooden cutouts of saints, intricately painted although faded by age.

These portals served to separate the congregation from the holy place, the sacred and profane. Between each painted relief was a wood panel carved into leafy vines. The beams that supported the structure were similarly carved with twining leaves.

In the center of the floor was a spindly wooden stool with a silver lantern sitting on top. On the right-hand side was a stark, wooden bench. To the left was a wooden bookstand. The Bible that would have been placed on it was not there. With that sober reminder of the political atmosphere, we left the church.

We spent several hours at the Village Museum. We wandered along winding paths that led us to old churches, mills, farmhouses, and workshops from the eighteenth and nineteenth centuries. Linden trees showered us in white blossoms as we passed.

We saw many peasant cottages, mostly with thickly thatched triangular roofs. The interiors had a few pieces of furniture and were decorated with local folk art and handcrafts. There were not many people at the museum, so most of the time we walked undisturbed. It was the first time since we had arrived in Romania that I felt normal. We did notice a number of soldiers who were obviously on leave—or were they? It was hard for us to say.

We left the museum and drove through the city looking for the commercial district. We were hungry and wanted to find a place to eat. It was time for us to attempt some interaction with the locals. Everywhere we looked there were piles of rubble. New buildings were in different stages of construction. Only a few months earlier,

Bucharest had experienced a 7.4 magnitude earthquake and fifteen hundred people had died. The evidence of the massive quake was everywhere.

The roads were lined with huge skyscraper-type apartment buildings. Whole sides of these buildings were gone, showing open rooms, smashed furniture, overturned mattresses, disconnected pipes and dangling electrical wiring. There must have been a vigorous cleanup of the rubble as all the roads were clear. But these gaping wounds in the buildings told the story of a terrible disaster. We could only imagine how the people were suffering. We were also mindful of the mosaic walls that lined the highway into the city.

We pulled onto a side street and parked near an area that appeared to have restaurants. We found that many were closed and the menus on the windows of others were impossible to read. We didn't feel confident enough to enter the darkened rooms. We eventually found a buffet style cafe with plate glass windows, which made it easier for us to look in. It was airy and welcoming.

We followed the customers in front of us. We picked up a tray, plate, and silverware, and rolled our trays along the rails in front of bins with various entrees. Most of the food was unidentifiable— sausages of unknown origin, vegetables that didn't resemble anything we were familiar with, and globs of green, white and yellow. Everything appeared greasy and nasty looking.

We chose a plate of stuffed green peppers. At the end of the line, a woman standing at an ancient cash register rang up our meal. We could read the white numbers on the machine and handed over the required amount. We waved off the change and she gave us a big grin. We sat in a booth near one of the windows. We realized that there were very few people dining. Although our lunch was greasy, it was tasty and we suffered no ill effects.

When we came out of the cafe, we noticed a long line of women snaked around the block across the street from us. What were they doing? Were they waiting for tickets of some kind? We kept on walking parallel to the line. At the end of the line, we were surprised to see that all these women were waiting to go into a supermarket. Those coming out of the market carried only one bag. After their hours of waiting, these women were only allowed to buy a rationed amount of food and other goods.

This was such a strange sight. Again we felt the oppression. There wasn't any sense of neighborhood or community, even though these women probably had stood together in line before and might know each other well. They weren't talking. They just stood patiently as if this were something they were accustomed to doing and knew they couldn't change. We wondered if it was because of that law that no more than four people could meet together. The women probably didn't want the Securitate to think they even knew each other.

Saddened, we walked back to the van hand in hand without speaking. The temperature had risen to the high nineties. Waves of heat shimmered on the road. We didn't have the heart to pretend to be tourists anymore.

We reported our day's activities to the guard at the campground entrance, which was pretty ridiculous. He didn't speak English. We just showed him the pamphlet from the museum and the receipts from the restaurant. He nodded and grinned. We took a chance anyway and told him in English where we went and what we did. He nodded and smiled at us, writing who knows what down on his clipboard. When he was finished, he waved his arm at us, as if to say we were free to go. We got back in the van and pulled into the same spot we had the night before.

"Well, that's one day done," Lon said to me, as he opened the van doors. "I think it went rather well, don't you?"

"When I wasn't looking over my shoulder, I actually enjoyed myself. It was quite interesting."

"Me, too. How about a game of hearts?"

Lon set up the table and I got out the cards. I put a pot of water on the stove and made some tea. We played cards until evening fell. We made a meal of peanut butter and jelly sandwiches before we pulled out the bed and prepared to sleep. It did not come quickly.

We talked about the children, how we first met, and our friends at the Shalom House. We talked about our faith and the number of ways God had made His presence known to us through the miraculous as well as the mundane. Eventually, our eyes closed and our minds calmed long enough to allow our dreams to take us into slumber.

The next morning, we woke up later than we had wanted. The sky was overcast with low hanging clouds. There was an ominous feel to the air as if a storm was brewing. Rather than see this as a bad omen, I thanked God for breaking the oppressive heat. We washed our faces, brushed our teeth and prepared for our second day as tourists in Bucharest.

We ate cold cereal with raisins and discussed the day's itinerary. We decided to go to the center of the city and walk around, seeing as much as possible. We would check out the churches and businesses and be as touristy as possible. Our plan made, we started up the van and drove back into the city.

We made our way to the Arcul de Triumf, circled it a few times and veered off onto a side street. We found a safe place to park and walked on the outside rim of the traffic circle, taking pictures of the official looking gray buildings. The cloud cover began to thin and occasional streaks of sunlight brightened the red flowers bordering the walkways. However, there really wasn't much to see, so we returned to the van and headed for the city center.

We drove past the Hotel Intercontinental, a white and gleaming structure rising many stories into the sky, and decided it would serve as a good landmark. It was the first five-star hotel in the city and was brand new. It was also near the National Theater and Bucharest University. We parked as soon as we could find a spot and walked back to the hotel. As we entered the lobby, it was as if we had walked into another country.

The interior was opulent even by European standards. It was a strange contrast to the poverty we had seen throughout the country and the city. Besides the native tongues of Yugoslavs and Romanians, we heard English, German and French spoken in the lobby. The people there were international businessmen and women and Eastern European tourists—most likely party officials.

The hotel furnishings were beautiful, new, and colorful. Large gilded mirrors on the walls reflected polished marble floors and the well-dressed people walking on them. Heavy printed curtains framed large windows and embroidered sheers muted the glare of the sun that was finally making an appearance.

The shops inside were like any to be found in a five-star hotel. As we poured through the information racks for a map, my ear caught the sound of American English. I scanned the room and located a well-dressed, middle-aged woman loudly exclaiming over a necklace in a shop window.

"But I want it!" she said. "Buy it for me!"

"But dear," her beleaguered male companion complained, "we'll have to declare it."

"I don't care about that. If you had to take me to this godforsaken country, the least you could do is buy me something worthwhile."

I watched as the man went into the jewelry store to purchase the necklace. I nudged Lon and we watched the necklace disappear from the window. Before long, the man returned with his package. The woman snatched it from his hand and stuffed it unceremoniously into a larger bag of previous purchases. She didn't appear to have received much joy from the lavish gift.

Before we turned away from the kiosk—our search for a map among the printed brochures fruitless—I heard the woman say, "Do we have to go outside? It's just so… so… primitive and dirty out there." Lon couldn't stand it any longer. He grabbed my arm and led me to the door. We were embarrassed to be from the same country as that woman. I had an inkling that another parable had been acted out in front of our eyes.

As we left the hotel, children besieged us, begging for coins and breaking my heart. There were so many of them. I looked for their parents and saw no one. They were like rats scurrying here and there, trying to get the advantage over each other, pushing and shoving.

One little girl came up to me and held out her grimy hand for a coin. She had long dirty brown hair and must have been six or seven. She was dressed in a filthy smock and had no shoes on. I noticed her other arm was bound against her side by a soiled cloth wrapping. She saw me look at it and quickly tore off the bandage to reveal a hideous infected wound that needed medical attention. She extended her hand, pleading without words.

I looked into her dark eyes. They were wild, haunted, desperate. I gasped. I gave her one of the Romanian leus I had in my pocket. I have no idea how much it was worth, but it started a near riot. The other children pushed her out of the way and swarmed around us, screaming for us to give them money. We threw coins on the ground and made our escape.

I couldn't bear to look back. From the sounds, I knew they were assaulting each other. It was an unsettling experience, and I couldn't help but cry. I felt sick to my stomach. Outside that opulent, surreal hotel with its facade of commerce and prosperity was a generation of children trapped in poverty and deep despair.

The government's grip on the people, and the deterioration of the economy, was creating a powder keg. Dangerous working conditions were leading to significant unrest. Later that year the coal miners in the Jiu Valley would go on a long strike. The Securitate would crush the opposition and become even more involved in the lives of the people, demanding that no more than three people meet at a time. This state of affairs continued until the revolution of 1989.

We had been walking for hours and it was hot. We were dying of thirst and needed to find something to drink. We were told not to drink any of the water because of the chance of contracting dysentery. We came to the entrance of a carnival. We could see rusty, paint-chipped amusement park rides in the enclosed space.

Aggressive barkers were practically dragging people to the ticket counter. We successfully avoided them and meandered through the various concession stands outside the fence. We saw some people buying a bottle of orange soda named CeCe from a tall, thin man in a long, ratty coat. Although he looked rather unsavory, the people seemed to enjoy the drink, so we bought two bottles for less than a leu. It was carbonated, sugary sweet and didn't taste much like orange, but it satisfied our thirst.

We slowly made our way into the residential sections. We stopped at little shops and bought small trinkets to justify our presence. We tried to appear to be innocent tourists, just scoping out interesting places. We didn't want our movements to seem strange once we had to go into the apartment complex of our contact.

We took a ride on the red and white tram to get the hang of paying the fare and sitting among the passengers. As long as we didn't speak, no one paid any attention to us. We felt confident we could pass for Romanians.

We also learned how to maneuver around the city. We were relieved to find that the tram stops had a big sign showing a map of the city. Although we couldn't take it back with us to Open Doors, we were able to find the street we needed. By the end of our long day, we knew where we were going and were ready to meet our secret contact. Tomorrow we would venture into the neighborhood where he was located.

We drove around the city, killing time until we came down a street that was closed for an open air market. There were a lot of people milling around the booths in the square. I rolled down the window. The smell of baked bread wafted inside the van and made my stomach growl.

"What do you think?" I asked. "Get some lunch and pick up some souvenirs?"

"Something to remember our trip, huh?" Lon said, agreeing with me. "After tomorrow, we'll be leaving Romania forever."

"You think we can risk doing a little shopping?"

He nodded. "I think we will be okay. We can park right over there."

"Let's pray God's protection over the van, and one of us needs to keep an eye on it the whole time."

We parked in front of a large box truck, put our hands surreptitiously on the van, prayed for protection and walked to the market. We followed our noses and immediately found the stall with the fresh bread. We purchased two long, crusty rolls and began munching on them as we strolled through the market. There were a number of stalls selling wilted greens and root vegetables. We passed them by, looking over our shoulders at the van.

Just past the vegetable stands, we encountered a woman who was sitting on a blanket with pottery and handcrafted items displayed all around her, incredible hand-painted pottery at pennies a piece. We filled our bags with many of them. At this point, I really felt like a tourist. I didn't even give a thought to what lay ahead of us until Lon touched my arm and pointed to his watch. It was time to do some reconnaissance.

We hauled our purchases back to the van and placed them in back on the floor. I felt a sudden stab of fear. What had we been thinking leaving the van in the middle of a marketplace? It was irresponsible! I expressed my feelings to Lon and he assured me that it could only have been the peace of God that had allowed us to have a completely peaceful afternoon.

We drove back to the campground as the sun began to set. We showed the guard our purchases and the pamphlets we got from the Hotel Intercontinental. He wrote it all down, nodding and grinning at the same time.

We pulled into our space, noticing that more tents were set up on the center lawn. We went to the shower room and freshened up, changing our clothes for the evening. That night we walked to a bistro we had noticed near the campground. It had an outdoor balcony, lights shining warmly in the mild evening air. We didn't say it, but I knew Lon was thinking the same—this was our last meal before we put our lives on the line.

A fat man in a black, soiled tuxedo ushered us to a small table on the balcony outside. He returned shortly with a basket of warm, fresh baked rolls. We looked at the menu. Thankfully there were pictures of the various dishes. Because Romania is a Latin-based language, we were able to decipher the entrees and we ordered. We also indulged in a carafe of wine—the safest thing to drink.

When our green salads were delivered, we took a roll, slathered it with creamy butter, and dug into our salads.

Lon grimaced. "I just ate something really bitter."

"What was it?" I asked, looking at my salad to see what was so unidentifiable. I was horrified to see a big green worm moving across my lettuce.

"I think I know what you just ate. Look."

Lon looked, grabbed his glass of wine and took a big gulp. He waved the waiter over and pointed at the giant worm in my salad. With no change in expression, the waiter bent down, closely peered at it, and then picked it up with his fingers and threw it over the railing. He bowed to us and left. We looked at each other and burst into laughter as we pushed our salad plates to one side.

Aside from the worm, our meals were very good. We toasted each other with our wine and laughed and talked as if we hadn't a care in the world. But underneath our gaiety, I was nervous. Every moment I felt like we were being observed. We probably were. The Securitate was so extensive, we couldn't know if we were under some level of observation. We had to make our time as tourists appear very believable. I shook off the foreboding and relaxed. I reminded myself that God was in control.

After our meal, Lon waved the waiter over for our bill. We muffled our giggles as he stood there and counted how many rolls we had consumed. There were only three left in the basket. He wrote down the damages and presented Lon with the bill. Lon looked at it.

"At least he didn't charge us for the worm," he said, grinning at me. We laughed until our sides hurt. We paid the bill and sauntered out of the restaurant.

It was a beautiful evening. We walked under flowering linden trees and inhaled their sweet scent. There were hardly any sounds except an occasional night bird cooing in the branches. I felt a deep peace steal over my soul and I knew that we were in the palm of God's hand.

# CHAPTER 10

# Foiled

The morning came in a bright light. The sun, just coming over the tree line in the campground, found its way around the curtains and onto our faces. This was the day we were to meet our contact. We put everything to rights in the van and dressed as conservatively as possible.

We had examined the way people dressed the day before and were somewhat surprised to see that the sixties were in fashion in Romania. Mini-skirts were everywhere. Still, Lon wore jeans and a plain blue shirt. I wore a blue blouse and a navy skirt. I put a kerchief on my head.

We checked out with the campground guard and smiled our goodbyes. I had a feeling he felt important having met Americans, and seemed sad to see us leave. Lon shook his hand, and then we climbed back into the van and left. We would not be returning.

We drove into the heart of Bucharest and looked for a safe place to park the van. After debating several locations, we settled on the parking lot of the Opera Nationala. We felt the camper van would not be noticed among the many other tourist vehicles. We would walk toward our designated street, stopping along the way at shops, constantly aware that Securitate could be signaling to others ahead of us.

There were thousands of paid informers in the city of Bucharest. If we warranted any curiosity, we would be endangering our contact. We were well aware that we had to become inconspicuous.

When we came to the street we sought, we hopped onto one of the trams, paid our fare and sat way in the back. We did not dare speak to one another and kept our eyes downcast. I glanced up a couple times to see if our presence was being observed, but as far as I could tell the people were absorbed in their own thoughts.

We rode the tram several blocks beyond our stop before getting off. We watched carefully to see if anyone got off with us. Three men and a woman disembarked. Two men crossed the tracks and headed to the other side. The woman went one way and the man went the other. We followed after the man to make sure he wasn't following us. When he went into an apartment building, we walked past to the end of the street and then turned around. The sidewalk was empty.

My husband grabbed my hand and we crossed the street. We walked another block to the next tram stop. We waited about ten minutes, joined only by a woman and her daughter. The young girl openly stared at us. Was it just the innocent curiosity of a child or did we stand out? I silently said another prayer. Her mother spoke to her, jerked her arm, and the child stopped staring.

The tram rumbled up and stopped. We stepped back to let the woman and her child step aboard. As I got on and paid the fare, Lon held back until the last minute and then jumped aboard. He paid his fare and guided me to a couple seats in the center of the tram. My heart was thudding. I caught his eye and he shook his head—in other words, no one had followed us.

The tram lumbered back the way we had come earlier, screeching at the stops. We watched people getting off and getting on. They were not unlike those I'd seen in New York or any other big city in America. The only difference was that there was no gaiety or chatter. They were somber and conversations were often in hushed tones. They were clean and neat, but their clothes had the look of long wear.

Girls giggled and teased their male companions. Businessmen stared in stony silence. Grandmothers scolded their grandchildren for fidgeting. Women with care-worn faces carried woven baskets for grocery shopping. All seemed so normal, but I was acutely aware that these people did not know freedom. They had learned to guard their talk and ideas. Suspicion and fear lay beneath the labors of everyday life.

Brother Andrew had warned us that things that could give us away were our countenance and our walk. Americans and other Westerners carried with them a self-assurance that was not found behind the Iron Curtain. While we had walked the streets the day before, I observed this phenomenon.

There was a hunched, slow gait to the Romanians. Their chins were stuck into their necks, or their heads hung down. Those who were probably "good Communists" walked more purposefully, but still didn't have the confidence that was commonplace in the West and it was said that Americans had even more of this confidence than the Europeans. Some might call it arrogance, but it was a birthright of liberty and the spirit of "Yankee" independence.

Lon pulled the cord before our tram stop. We kept our eyes downcast, but he took my hand and gave it a squeeze. The tram screeched to a stop. We got up and moved to the exit. We waited our turn as three people ahead of us got off.

Suddenly, just as we were leaving the tram, a man jumped up and got off behind us. Lon took my hand and pulled me across the street. The man followed us. Instead of going down the street to where our destination lay, we went up the street. We slowed our walk, hoping the man would pass us. He stayed behind us and seemed to be pacing himself with us. We kept walking. My heart was in my throat, and I expected at any moment that he would lay his hands on us.

Just as I was thinking this, Lon stopped and pulled off his tennis shoe. He spent a considerable time trying to get an imaginary rock out of his shoe. The man passed us. I stole a glance after him. He did not alter his stride in any way but kept moving. Lon put his shoe back on and stood up. He watched until he was satisfied that there was nothing sinister about the man.

"Come on," he said, taking my hand.

We retraced our steps to the tram stop, crossed the street and walked in the opposite direction. The street numbers were painted on the sidewalk curbs. We were getting close. The street was lined on both sides with ten-story, concrete apartment buildings. They all looked exactly the same. There was no color, showed no sense of community and no outward sign of individuality. It was an oppressive street, exactly the same as every other residential street that we had observed in Bucharest.

We came to the street number and walked up a short flight of stairs to the front glass doors of the apartment building. There was an old, rotund man standing against the railing near the doors, smoking. He had a flat cap on his head and wore a bulky navy coat. His dirty white shirt hung halfway out of his baggy pants. He stared at us. I avoided eye contact. Lon nodded, and we brushed past him through the doors and into a foyer.

Mercifully there was an elevator and we did not encounter anyone else. He punched the button to the tenth floor and up we went. The elevator moved at the slowest pace that was possible. I prayed that no one would enter the elevator as it crawled upwards.

Finally, the doors opened on the tenth floor. We cautiously stepped out. The hallway was empty. We walked down the hallway until we came to number 108. We held both hands and bowed in prayer. "Lord, protect us and our contact." We hugged and kissed each other. Lon knocked on the door. We waited. He knocked again. No answer. He put his ear to the door.

"I can't hear anything," he whispered to me.

"They can't be gone!"

"I don't think anyone's there," he said.

"But they've got to be!"

He knocked again. We waited, but no one came to the door. I felt panic rise and I fought it. God was in control. He would see us through this. Don't panic!

He shrugged his shoulders. "Come on. They're not here. We'll get some lunch and come back later."

We rode the elevator back to the first floor without incident. The old man was still standing against the railing outside. He continued to stare at us but did not speak. With heavy hearts, we walked back to the tram stop and waited. Before long the tram arrived and we stepped on. We rode in silence, our thoughts racing as to what our next move should be. As soon as we came into sight of a row of restaurants and shops we pulled the cord and got off.

We stopped at an open-air cafe. We ordered bread, cheese, and coffee. We sat in silence, absorbed in thought. We had come so far, only to be thwarted at the critical juncture. I felt like crying.

My husband's hand touched mine and I looked up. He smiled at me and I felt ashamed. How pitiful was my faith! This was not in my hands. I did not control what was happening. I was completely in His care. I had to trust God and not be afraid.

"I thought that guy was following us, didn't you?" Lon said.

"Until he passed us. I thought I was going to faint."

"Maybe he was. Think about it. Maybe that's why we didn't make contact."

"What do you mean?" I asked, revelation slowly coming.

"I mean we have to believe God is with us. He is protecting us. He knows the best time for us to make contact. There's a reason why they're not at home."

"I hadn't thought of that, but you could be right. We shouldn't be discouraged because our first attempt was unsuccessful."

"There's no way we could have entered this country like we did if God wasn't with us."

I smiled and my heart lightened. "That's true. I'm sorry I doubted."

"We're not there yet, but I believe it will happen today. Let's just enjoy our lunch. You have to admit this is pretty nice."

"Like Paris."

"Yes, just like Paris. This bread is really good."

"And the butter tastes so sweet and creamy."

"And, I think this might just be the best coffee I've ever had."

"I think you're right. Try this cheese."

The rest of our lunch took on the atmosphere of pure joy. I felt the Spirit of Peace fill my being. I felt Love all around me. It was almost gauzy the way the Holy Spirit surrounded us. It was like a force field.

At that moment I felt as if someone could shoot a gun at us and it would not penetrate the protection of God. Strength filled my body. Where I had felt completely depleted, drained of energy, I now felt renewed in body and spirit.

We paid for our lunch with three leu bills and received fifty bani in return. I wanted to leave it as a tip, but Lon reminded me that was a Western custom. Money was too scarce for the Romanians to lavish it about. I felt so filled with the love of the Holy Spirit that I insisted.

As the waiter came to clear the table, Lon slipped the fifty bani coins into his hand. The man's eyes widened as he looked at the coins in his hand. We smiled at him and his face broke into a big grin. He grabbed and pumped Lon's hand, saying something to us, which I assumed was "thank you very much". We nodded and Lon pulled his hand from the man's grasp.

We walked away down the street. I looked back once and the waiter was still standing there, watching us. He raised his hand. I gave him a little wave and rushed to catch up with my husband.

# CHAPTER 11

# Contact

We returned to our contact's apartment after repeating our previous jumping on and off the tram, watching for suspicious activity. This time, no one appeared to follow us and strangely the street seemed to be deserted. The old man was no longer at the doorway, and we went into the elevator without being observed.

We walked down the hallway to number 108 and again knocked on the door. We waited. No answer. Lon knocked again, giving me a thumb's up and a smile. The door opened a crack, and we could see half of a woman's face.

"Dr. Constantinescu?" Lon said quietly. "Open Doors."

The door opened and an arm shot out, grabbed his arm, and pulled him inside. I followed; the door was shut quickly behind us. The woman was short and slim, wearing a faded yellow dress. I guessed her age at forty. Her hands clasped each side of her face and her eyes looked scared. She began speaking in rapid Romanian, beckoning us into the sitting room.

"Dr. Constantinescu?" Lon asked. "Is he here?"

She violently shook her head and began pacing, still speaking rapidly. She stopped and gestured for us to sit on a low couch. We sat and tried to make progress with communication.

"Brother Andrew sent us," Lon said. "We need to speak to Dr. Constantinescu. Is he here?"

"No," she said, waving her arm. He's away, she seemed to be indicating.

Lon looked at me, perplexed. "He's not here. We're going to have to find the alternate contact."

I got up and took the woman by the arm and led her to a chair. She sat and fidgeted, like a captured bird. I felt great compassion for her. I knelt down beside her, pulled my cross from beneath my blouse and pointed to it. "Jesus," I said. "Jesu Christo." She clasped it between her hands and nodded.

"Do you speak any English?" I asked. "English?"

She shook her head no.

"*Deutsch? Sprechen ze Deutsch?*" I asked if she spoke German. I was hoping we could find common ground. Perhaps this was why I had felt the need to exercise my German when we were in Köln.

"*Ja. Ich sprechen Deutsch*," she said, nodding that she spoke German, and for the first time, smiled.

"*Ich sprechen un betchen Deutsch*," I said, meaning I spoke a little German.

For the next twenty minutes, she and I conversed in halting German. God gave me the words and the understanding to communicate with her. I learned that she was Nadia Constantinescu and her husband, Emil, was away traveling, and would not be back for a week. We would not be able to wait that long.

I conveyed to her that we had a "shipment" from Open Doors. She understood what I was saying and began to cry. She started speaking rapidly in her native tongue, placing her hands on my head. She hugged me and her tears marked my face. I realized she was crying for joy. I started crying, too.

"What's going on?" Lon asked.

I turned to him and told him what I had learned.

"Ask her where and when we should make the transfer?"

I did my best, but it was soon apparent to all of us that with our limited language skills we would not be able to make detailed plans for the delivery of the Bibles. This would be the most dangerous part of the mission. We both grew frustrated with trying to communicate. We finally gave it up. We were at a stalemate.

"Let's pray," Lon said. We all held hands. "Lord Jesus," he prayed aloud, "we know that in your infinite wisdom that you know what is happening here. You know that your persecuted church is desperate for these Bibles and that we must find a way to make this work. We put ourselves in your hands and ask for your help. Help us, Lord Jesus. Help us find a way. Amen."

When he finished, Nadia indicated that we should wait for her. She disappeared down a hallway. Lon and I were nervous. Again, things had not gone as planned. Here we had overcome insurmountable obstacles to find our way in the capital city of Bucharest to the apartment of our contact, only to find he was not there.

It was part of the faith ministry of Open Doors. It was impossible to know or communicate when the Bibles would arrive. All the contact knew was that someday a courier would arrive, say "Open Doors," and the Bibles would be transferred to them. Unfortunately for us, our contact would not return for a week.

Shortly, Nadia returned. She put on a coat. She picked up her purse and indicated to us that we were leaving. She put her finger on our lips and shook her head. We understood and reassured her that we would not say a word.

She slowly opened the door, looked into the hallway, and then stepped out. We followed her. We headed to the elevator and my heart skipped a beat as a door opened and a man and woman came out of an apartment. They spoke with Nadia in a casual way, looking at us with curiosity. I don't know what she told them, but when we all entered the elevator they didn't say anything more.

She ushered us out of the building and down the steps. Just as we came to the street a taxi pulled up. Lon opened the back door for me. Nadia pushed me in and scooted in beside me. She indicated to Lon that he was to sit up front. He acquiesced and got into the passenger seat. We learned later that it would have been considered improper for her to sit next to a man who was not her husband, or to have a man sit in back while she sat in front.

She spoke rapidly to the taxi driver. He jerked the vehicle into the street and sped off. He roared through intersections, slammed on his brakes as a tram sliced its way in front of us, then he was off again. I clung to the edge of my seat, bumping against Nadia several times.

I could see Lon was hanging on to the dashboard. The driver was a maniac. He screeched around a corner and raced down a street. As we came to a congested intersection, he laid on his horn. His actions terrified us. Don't call attention to us, I screamed silently.

He jerked the wheel toward the sidewalk and to our surprise and horror plowed onto the sidewalk and drove around a traffic jam, with pedestrians scurrying out of his way. He clipped some garbage cans, sending them spilling into the street.

Racing down another street, he dodged a truck as it came out of an alleyway, barely missing it. He took a turn down another side street and then came out into a larger intersection. A black sedan came out of nowhere and headed straight at us. At the last minute, he swerved to avoid it. To our horror, the black car clipped the fender of the taxi, spun around and came to a stop.

Our taxi driver did not stop or slow down. Instead, he gunned the engine and raced down several more streets. He slowed as he entered traffic around the Arcul de Triumf in the center of Bucharest. He circled around it several times, maneuvering through the traffic lanes, whether to avoid detection or to calm our frazzled nerves, I will never know.

Suddenly, another black sedan roared up beside us and cut us off. Our driver slammed on his brakes, sending us flying against the front seats. He swore profusely in Romanian until Nadia reached over the seat and hit his arm. He looked chagrined, ground the gears and moved across several lanes of traffic away from the black sedan.

Nadia was mumbling under her breath. I assumed she was praying, so I joined her. I reached my hand up to Lon's shoulder and gave him a squeeze. He placed his hand over mine but dared not look back at me. His eyes were fixed on the road ahead.

Our driver moved to the right across three lanes and eventually dove down a side street. He took several turns gradually slowing down and driving at what seemed more like a normal rate of speed.

After what felt like an hour, he pulled the taxi over and stopped. Nadia spoke to him. I did not see any money change hands before she got out and opened the doors for us. We could only wonder if this taxi driver was a relative or member of the underground church, and what he would say to his boss about the dents in the fender.

Nadia indicated we needed to hurry. She rushed up the stairway, entering another apartment building. This one was not as sterile as the others we had seen. It was more classical-looking with concrete scrolls and an arch above the doors. We walked up a flight of stairs. She knocked on the door and a woman opened it. She pushed us inside and turned to the woman, closing the door. We stood there stupidly as the two women conversed.

The other woman kept glancing at us. We could see it dawning on her who we were and why we were there. She suddenly broke away from Nadia and surprised us by hugging us both, her eyes glistening with unshed tears. She ushered us into her sitting room, speaking graciously to us. She had us sit at a table and asked us to wait. She and Nadia left the room.

"What's going on?" Lon asked me.

"I have no idea," I replied. "I think she's a friend, maybe someone in the underground church. I think her name is Elika. She has to be a Christian otherwise why would Nadia bring us here."

"I thought we were goners there for a minute," he said, adjusting his bottom on the ladder-back chair.

"I've never been so scared in my life," I said.

"Did you see that black sedan that cut us off? Do you think it was the same one that clipped us?"

"How could it be?"

"Didn't Brother Andrew tell us that only senior Communist party officials drove black sedans?"

"You don't think… " I gasped, thinking of our harrowing ride.

Was there more danger ahead? Had we been discovered?

"Maybe. What do we know? We're in these women's hands. I sure hope they know what they're doing."

"We're also in God's hands. He knows," I said, reassuring myself as well as him.

"You're right. I think I saw Jesus during that cab ride."

I giggled as the tension began to lessen in my shoulders.

The women returned, carrying crystal mugs filled with clear liquid. They set the two mugs in front of us. Inside the glass was a spoon with a big glob of pink on it. They were very pleased to offer it to us. We looked at each other, then at them. They were beaming and nodding.

"What are we supposed to do with this?" Lon whispered.

"Drink it, I guess."

We lifted the mugs to our lips and sipped, moving the spoon out of the way. It was sweet water. When we set the mugs down we thanked them. They indicated that we were to eat from the spoon. We picked up the spoon and took a nibble of the pink goo. It was pure sugar, probably the sweetest thing I had ever tasted.

I smiled up at them and said, "mmm." Turning to my husband, I asked, "Lon, do you know what this is?"

"Regurgitated cotton candy?"

"It's sugar candy. Remember, they told us there was a sugar shortage in Romania. People spend hours in line just to get a cup of sugar. This is a great sacrifice for Elika. She is showing us how grateful she is to give this up for us."

"I get that, but it's killing my fillings."

"We can't be rude. Act like you like it."

We thanked them again and nibbled on the sugary goo and sipped the water. We made appreciative smacking noises. They were at last satisfied that their precious gift was well received. Mrs. Constantinescu sat at the table and spoke to me in German.

"We know a man who speaks English. He is at our church. We will take you to him when it is safe," she said.

I translated for Lon.

"Fantastic. When?"

I asked her when we would go. She told me that we had to wait for their friends to come. Then we would go. It was not safe yet.

As time went by, we watched from our chairs in the sitting room as more people arrived. They gave us furtive glances, but no one came to speak to us. There were conversations in hushed tones with occasional glances our way. As odd as it seemed, I felt their love. They were scared, careful, but incredibly excited.

It came as a shock to me to realize that Lon and I were like angels in their midst. They were awestruck by our presence. They saw us as an answer to their continual, fervent prayers; prayers of deep faith from people who had given their lives to Christ.

It was not just words with them—it was a faith that came from seeing their members jailed, confined to insane asylums, killed; their children taken from them, and subjected to unspeakable terrors of the flesh. That was a faith of which we in the West had no understanding. We had never suffered such persecution.

We were their hope, and we had arrived. Tears came to my eyes as I realized how they saw us. I was humbled and felt deeply unworthy. I shared my thoughts with Lon and he nodded, tears pricking his eyes. He realized it, too. This was why we had agreed to do this mission. We were the answer that God had provided to them.

We could not, God help us, would not fail.

# CHAPTER 12

## Passing the Test

A couple hours passed before the people in Elika's apartment determined that it was safe to move us. I noticed a tall, thin man with a goatee. He wore a cap on his head, a tweed blazer with a scarf around his neck. He did not smile or even really look at us.

He didn't speak to us but seemed to be arguing with Elika. I began to suspect that he was her husband. Nadia joined in the agitated conversation. I don't think he wanted us in his house.

I looked at Lon and could see that he thought the same. The pink goo was starting to give me a headache, and I didn't think I would be able to finish it. Would they be insulted if I left a little on my spoon?

Eventually, Nadia brought the silent man over to us. After all these years, I have to admit that I don't remember his name. His face is imprinted on my mind because I could tell he was highly suspicious of us. He held out his hand palm up. We looked at each other and back to him. Nadia came over and said, "*Reispässe.*" I did not know the word.

"*Paşaport,*" the man said urgently in Romanian. That I understood.

"He wants to see our passports," I said, my stomach contracting.

"No problem," Lon said, smiling up at the stern man. We pulled out our passports and gave them to him. Nadia looked at them over his shoulder.

"*Amerikaner!*" she exclaimed. I never realized until that moment that they didn't know we were Americans. It appeared to make us even more of a miracle.

The man barely registered his surprise, nodded curtly, handed our passports back, and indicated we were to leave together. I picked up the spoon and sucked off the rest of the pink goo and washed it down with the water. Lon grinned at me and showed me his empty spoon. It was just the right touch at that moment when I was feeling nervous. We stood as people began to leave the apartment.

The first to go were a man and woman. They came over and shook our hands before they left, smiling shyly. Ten minutes later, two young women left, glancing at us from the door, faces shining with hero-worship as if we were celebrities. They were hustled out the door by a man who touched his cap as he left. Five minutes after them, two older men gave us a nod and left.

Eventually, Nadia came over to us.

"You go with them," she told me in German, pointing to Elika and her man.

I was sorry to see her leave. After five minutes, the silent man, who I began to suspect was our host, indicated with his head that we were to leave, too. I was suddenly afraid. What if this was a set-up? What if we had been betrayed? We didn't know this man. I wanted to stay with Mrs. Constantinescu. She was our contact's wife. Sensing my fear, Lon took my hand and squeezed it as if to say, "it's okay."

Elika joined us, pulling a scarf over her head. She gave us a reassuring smile, shook her husband's arm as if to say, "lighten up," and opened the door. We were to walk behind them as we left the apartment.

Night had descended while we were in the apartment. There were no street lamps. It was so dark outside, I could barely see across the street. I held tightly onto Lon's arm. The couple led us to a small white car. It was a Dak. It had only two gears: forward and reverse. We squeezed into the back seat as the couple got into the front.

They drove carefully and slowly through the streets. I noticed that they meandered through a number of roads. At one point, they appeared to drive completely around the block. I was beginning to realize that this was their way of making sure the Securitate wasn't following.

We drove into another darkened neighborhood and then Elika's husband pulled the car over. They got out. He opened the door for us and again jerked his head to indicate we were to follow him. We walked down the street to a dead end. We stood in front of a seven-foot wooden fence, but I could see a large, three-story house behind it. There were lights in one of the windows at the top. The man knocked a series of raps and the gate of the fence was opened.

We entered an extensive overgrown garden. The door of the house opened and light streamed out onto the sidewalk where we stood. I could see the lawn more clearly now and it looked as if it had once been beautiful, but was now neglected and shabby.

People started coming out of the house and down the steps toward us. Before we knew what was happening, we were surrounded. The man who had brought us stood on Lon's side and Elika stood at my side. She had her arms crossed, but one hand clasped my arm and held me close. Nadia stood next to her. I smiled at her, but she wouldn't look at me.

A man came up to Lon, put his hands on his shoulders and looked at him, then moved on to me and did the same. His gaze was intense. I smiled at him and said hello. He said nothing but moved on. Then a woman followed. She stared at Lon, and then stared at me. Then another man did the same, then another, on and on, until it seemed like ten or more people had stood before us and stared at us without saying anything.

I didn't know what was going on, but as people came and went they clustered in groups around us, speaking softly to each other. I could feel a growing excitement. Finally, the last man stood in front of us. He was about Lon's height. He had kind, light eyes, was clean-shaven, and he smiled a gentle smile that eased my anxiety. He took Lon's hand and mine in his.

"Do not be afraid," he said in English. "They see Jesus in your eyes. They know you not Securitate. I am Teodor. Welcome to our church. You have something for us?"

We nodded and followed him up the stairs into the house. The crowd of people did not follow as we climbed another flight of stairs. I watched as those behind us walked down a hallway and entered a very large living room, ablaze with light. My last sight of the underground church in Romania was the flickering shadows of many hands lifted up in praise before the doors of the room closed.

I returned my attention to Teodor, who led us up six flights of stairs. The house was obviously the home of someone of means. I got a strong impression from the heavy, dark, antique furniture and the quality of the porcelain bowls and figurines set on accent tables at each landing that this was someone's ancestral home. How it had become the location for the underground church was a story I would soon learn.

The last flight of stairs was very narrow, and we filed up to a door. Teodor knocked softly. It slowly opened. There was a quick whispered conversation before we moved forward and entered into an upstairs apartment.

"This is Elisabet," Teodor said.

The woman who greeted us was very old. Her milky white eyes revealed her blindness, but she clasped our hands in hers and welcomed us in her native tongue. Her hands were warm and dry.

She was a tall woman with a slight stoop. I estimated her age at close to eighty.

Her hair was pure white and plaited in two braids wrapped onto the top of her head like a crown. Her face was creased with deep wrinkles, except around her eyes. She was dressed in a blue blouse and long blue skirt with a navy apron that hung to the floor, revealing round toed, sturdy brown shoes beneath. She gave me a dry kiss on each cheek. Her rosy cheeks were as soft as fine velvet. She whispered something in my ear.

She beckoned us into her parlor. It was very warm in the apartment. I was pleased to see Nadia and her friend Elika. They gave us a quick hug of welcome. They turned to Elisabet and spoke to her, answering her questions.

I could see that Teodor and the two women revered this old woman, showing her deference as they moved a large overstuffed chair near a table and helped her to sit in it. They indicated two straight-backed chairs at the table for us. As we sat down, our guides moved away, speaking rapidly in whispers to each other.

The old woman sat with a beatific smile on her face. Her hands were clasped in her lap. She neither spoke nor looked around, and I could only assume that she was listening to her fellow Christians.

While our companions were absorbed in their conversation, I took the opportunity to look around the room. A round hooked rug spanned the floor of the parlor. There was a low couch with wood armrests against one wall. The upholstery was a faded flower pattern with two back and two bottom cushions. There was a beautiful antique china cabinet on the wall opposite where I was sitting, and I could see fine china and knickknacks inside. Next to it was an ornate chiffonier, covered by a linen cloth. Upon it was a Greek Orthodox cross and a grouping of old photos in frames. I wanted to get up and look at the photos but felt rooted to my seat, excited and expectant about what would come next.

I glanced at our companions. They were deep in a discussion. I let my gaze wander to the next room. It was an efficiency kitchen. I could see cupboards, a sink, and a counter with a double hot plate on the counter with a teakettle and a pot on it.

There was a lot of clutter in the kitchen and the smell of something sour wafted to my nostrils. I could see a plate with morsels of food sitting on the counter, and I wondered if we had interrupted the old woman's dinner. Across the table, I saw two closed doors that I assumed were bedrooms, but I couldn't tell what else might be on this floor.

My gaze returned to Elisabet who sat placidly and without movement. She seemed to emit a strange glow. I rubbed my eyes and looked again. I was not mistaken. There was light all around her. I looked behind me for the source of the light, but the windows were heavily curtained. In the dim light of the room, the old woman emitted a light of her own. My heart leaped within me as I realized it was a halo. I was in the presence of a saint.

Just as this idea came to me, our companions broke up their conversation and hovered around the old woman. The two other women spoke to her in soft undertones. She nodded. She lifted her hands and placed them on their bowed heads. She raised her blind eyes toward heaven and began to pray. I bowed my own head, knowing that God would hear the prayers of this old woman.

"Help me," Teodor said to my husband.

He proceeded to remove all the crockery and candles from the table, and they folded up the handcrafted crocheted table covering. He handed it to the women. He then pulled out a folded paper from his coat and laid it out on the table. It was a hand drawn map of the city. Lon and I looked at each other.

"Show me where," he said.

The two women drew close to the table and looked down on the map as if they could envision the Bibles hidden inside our van. We both stood up. Lon turned the map toward him and examined it. He was blessed with an incredible sense of direction and was able to trace our entrance into Bucharest and locate the Opera Nationala where we had parked the van.

"Good, good!" Teodor said. "Tomorrow night. Do you have watch? Good. Start there. You be here at half seven, before sun go down," he pointed to a spot on the map.

We all bent over to examine the chosen location and where it was in relation to the Opera House.

"See? You drive here, then here; you see grey building with black metal fence, turn after you pass, then go straight for five kilometers," Teodor said, his voice low and intense. "You see white building made of stone on hill. It was church, but now…"

He struggled to come up with a word, shrugged, and settled on, "no more."

At this point the women began to speak rapidly. He replied, confirming what they said, and they nodded. He looked back at us and smiled.

"Nadia and Elika wait for you on side of road at the… end… of the hill."

He made a sloping gesture with his hand and indicated the base of the hill. We nodded in understanding.

"Park behind car, white Dak," he continued. "They go for walk. You wait for they return. If good, Nadia will… (he pursed his lips and whistled a little tune), take off sweater and put on her arm, this arm," he grasped her left arm and raised it up high.

They laughed together, suddenly giddy, until their decorum returned with a glance at the old woman. She smiled and nodded, and Teodor continued. "They get in car and you go after. They take you to place… you give… us… Bibles… understand?"

We nodded. He was almost overcome with emotion, and wiped his eyes with a handkerchief. "You not know where it is. Just follow. Stay close. Understand?"

We nodded. He became even more serious as he looked us in the eyes. "But, if not good, Nadia no (he whistled). No take off sweater. They go by, get in car and go away. You wait five (he held up five fingers), and go away. Fast! Understand?"

We nodded solemnly. I felt suddenly sick to my stomach. I looked up and caught the blind gaze of the old woman. She appeared to be looking right at me. She smiled and nodded and I felt suddenly at peace. "Thank you," I mouthed to her.

"God no bring you here for Securitate. You answer our prayers. God is with you."

"We believe that, too," Lon said. "We will be there tomorrow. Nothing will stop us. The Lord will have His way, and you will have your Bibles. Have faith."

He stuck his hand out and Teodor shook it firmly. The two men hesitated, and then hugged.

"Teodor, do you mind if I ask questions?" He broke the embrace and turned to me. He gave me a kind, indulgent smile and nodded. "Where is Dr. Constantinescu?" I asked.

"I don't know. Nadia say he away. He profesor universitar. We not know you come. He sad no see you. He told us. Be ready. We tell him about you."

"And, if you don't mind, who is she?" I asked timidly, indicating the old woman.

He smiled broadly. "She is mother of our church. Her man begin church thirty year after *purifica* [pogrom]. Many *ministru* [ministers and priests] put in camps. The true church no more. Christians hide their faith. Elisabet and Janos make house secret church. They put Janos in prison, but he stay Christian. Three time he go to prison. Last time he very sick. He die. Elisabet keep church open."

At her name, the old woman looked up. Everyone looked at her. I glanced at Teodor, Nadia and Elika. Their love for her was evident. She made a move to get up, and Nadia and Elika rushed to assist her. She stood, spoke a few words, and opened her arms.

"She wants to pray for you," Teodor said, moving out of the way and pulling me toward her.

We willingly went into the old woman's arms. She embraced us and began to pray. Her voice grew stronger the longer she prayed. The Spirit of God filled the room and I was transported to the bright, warm throne room of God. My body tingled with an intense energy. I felt Lon's fingers grasp mine as Elisabet prayed over us.

It was not until she finished speaking that I realized that the other three also had their arms around us. I cannot fully describe the aura in the room. Everything seemed covered in a warm glow, the edges of the room fuzzy and soft.

As we broke apart, the aura clung to us, but the room took on its normal view and we knew it was time to leave. I could see Elisabet was tired. As we filed out of her apartment and back down the stairs, I turned and hugged her once more.

She whispered again in my ear, laying her dry, hot hand on the top of my head. I believe her blessing still covers me.

# CHAPTER 13

## Vulnerable

Teodor drove us back to our camper van at the opera house and said goodbye. We asked him if we could keep the map, but he said no. He explained it was too dangerous for us to be found with a map of the city. As disappointed as we were, we understood. I hugged him and we said goodbye once again. It would be the last time we would ever see each other and the moment was not lost on any of us.

We watched him leave before we got into the van. It was very late and we were exhausted. The tension from the day had begun to take its toll. We sat in the back of the van and discussed what we should do.

The most dangerous part of our mission lay just ahead. Given that Teodor's plan required that we be at our rendezvous point in the early evening of the next day, we would have to remove the Bibles from their hiding place either sometime during the next day or that very night. We had no idea how long this would take, but once we opened the panels and removed the hidden Bibles we would be at our most vulnerable. If we removed the Bibles that night, we would have to leave them exposed for a whole day before we could put them into the hands of our Romanian brethren. It was a dilemma.

"I don't like the idea of driving around with the Bibles out in the open for a whole day," I said. "But Brother Andrew did it."

"He had a handful of Bibles. We've got five thousand. Plus, we have no idea how long it's going to take to remove them," Lon said, rubbing his eyes and looking exhausted.

"Did the guy from Open Doors show you how they were stashed in there?" I asked.

"No. In fact, I have no idea how they hid so many in this camper van. I expect it's going to take us some time to get them out."

"Well, if we do it tomorrow, we'll need to do it outside the city. It's too busy here. Too many eyes," I argued.

"I agree," he said. "We'll drive out of the city, take out the Bibles, and meet them at the rendezvous point."

"How long do you think we'll need?"

"I think it's going to be at least a couple hours."

"We can't afford to be late, " I reminded him. "They'll think something went wrong and leave. Then what will we do?"

"We can do it in the morning and be ready in plenty of time."

"If we're going to have them out in the open all day anyway, I'd rather do it tonight." My head hurt just thinking about what I was saying.

"It might be best to do it under the cover of darkness. We could go back to the campground and... "

"Not there. We already checked out. Don't you think the guard will be suspicious, and what about all the people camping next to us? Won't they wonder what we're doing?"

"You're right," he agreed. "So what are we going to do?"

"Let's pray. God knows how He wants this to go down."

After spending some time in prayer, we decided to remove the Bibles that night, but not in the campground. We would look for the perfect location. We drove out of the parking lot of the Opera Nationala and through the dark streets of Bucharest.

As we passed the Arcul de Triumf, the circle around it blazed with lights as car headlights whizzed around the monument. It was quite beautiful, and I suddenly wished I were just a tourist instead of a smuggler. Its beauty dimmed as the lights seemed to change into a million prying eyes bent on our discovery. I shook my head and prayed.

"Where are we going?" I asked Lon, growing more anxious as we drove through the city. "We need to be out of sight, someplace where we won't be noticed."

"We can't keep driving around forever," he snapped. Tension was mounting. Our nerves were frayed and the longer we drove, the more irritable we became.

"Look, over there. How 'bout there?" he said, pointing.

"Where?"

"There. There!"

I saw what he saw. "Yes! Go!"

At the last minute, he swung the camper van into an empty lot surrounded by fields and edged by a wire fence. The nearest building was a brew house that was still open. Its blue neon sign flashed *Casa Escu* on the few cars parked next to it.

He pulled the camper parallel to the fence line and stopped. With the fields surrounding us on two sides, the only view of our van was from the street. We waited, watching the street for quite awhile. Several cars went by.

Would the Securitate or one of their myriad informers see us and wonder what we were doing? Would someone tell the police that we were hanging out in a vacant lot? As tourists, we were only allowed to stay overnight in official campgrounds. We were breaking the law by "camping out" in a parking lot.

We were running out of time.

"Let's do it," I said.

We climbed into the back and pulled all the curtains shut. I once again put up the curtain behind the front seats. Saying a prayer as he worked, Lon removed the necessary barrier and located the release lever. He gave me an encouraging smile and pulled the lever. We heard a loud clunk. The sound echoed in the quiet night. I peeked out the back curtain. We were apparently undetected and alone.

"Get the garbage bags," Lon whispered.

I ducked into the front and looked for the bags stored under the front seat. At first I couldn't find them, but eventually I located the roll of black plastic bags and pulled them out. By the time I returned, Lon already had the floorboard panel lifted and the side panels removed.

Since the Bibles had been packed into the van before we picked it up, this was our first look at the gift for which we were risking our lives. On the sides, they were stacked vertically, three deep, one on top of the other—packed solid. With the floorboards removed, the contraband was revealed. These were not Bibles, but songbooks, filled with hymns of praise and supplication. They had bright red covers. I had a sudden vision of Romanian Christians—men, women and children—holding these red books and singing praises to God. I got a lump in my throat just thinking about it.

Lon cleared his throat and I was reminded that we didn't have much time. I got busy. We worked steadily, prying books from beneath the floor. Hidden in the deepest recess, Lon pulled out several cans of printer's ink.

As I took the quart-sized cans from him and placed them in a plastic bag, they were hot in my hands. Not only had they absorbed the heat from the van, but also they were hot property—a dangerous weapon. Anyone, not just Christians, who got their hands on printer's ink was capable of fueling sedition. This would not be easy to explain away if we were caught with them in our possession.

A rumble and the sound of crunching gravel froze us where we knelt. We looked at each other with wide eyes. What was that? Lights suddenly glared through the slits in the curtains, revealing the bag full of songbooks and the hole in the floor, still containing more songbooks.

My heart began thrumming as my pulse quickened. I saw sweat on Lon's forehead. Had we been caught? I moved the curtain aside slowly and looked out, expecting to see our camper van surrounded by police cars, blue lights flashing. What I saw amazed me.

A huge tour bus circled the vacant lot and pulled alongside us, paralleling our van, and blocking any view of us from the street. With a squeal of brakes and a grumble from the engine being cut, the lights went out. We watched in breathless silence as, one by one, tourists filed out of the bus, laughing and talking, and headed across the vacant lot toward *Casa Escu*. Nothing could look more ordinary. Still, we held our breaths and tried not to move.

After five minutes, everyone had left, even the bus driver, and we were now completely hidden from view. We hugged each other and began praising God. We had been given perfect protection. There was no way anyone could see us from the street. All they would see was a large tour bus. We would be able to remove all the

Bibles without any fear of being discovered. We figured we would have at least a good hour before the tourists returned. We quickly got to work.

Lon sat up, his arms scraped raw and his breathing heavy. "That's all in here," he said, pulling the panels over to cover the hole in the floor and laying down the floorboards. "Let's get to the side panels."

"We've got to be methodical about this," I said, sitting on the bag with the ink cans in it. "We're running out of space and we haven't even pulled out the Bibles."

"You're right," he said, looking around. "We can't very well risk opening the door and putting them on the ground while we pull out the rest of the Bibles."

"We might if we hurry. As long as the bus shields us, we have protection."

"I'm not ready to do that. Let's see how it goes," he said, pulling a Bible out and holding it in his hand. It was about six inches high and four inches wide with a black cover. It looked like an ordinary book, but we knew inside it was anything but ordinary.

I opened a large trash bag and Lon began pulling out the Bibles one at a time from the hiding place and stuffing them inside. I joined him. They were packed tight and we had to wiggle and pull them from between the struts with our fingers, being careful not to tear the pages or the binding. These Bibles would get a lot of wear. I imagined them being passed from hand to hand and hidden in small cramped spaces.

The work was slow and tiring and we worked at a feverish pace. When one trash bag was filled, we moved it to the front and filled another. When we had pulled all the Bibles from that side, we lifted the panel from the other side and began pulling them out of every nook and cranny. We had to crawl over the bags to get to the left side. Five thousand Bibles and twenty-five hundred songbooks create a lot of volume.

"We're going to have to open the back door," Lon said, now unable to reach the Bibles because of all the bags in his way. My heart sank. We had been at this for over an hour, but the tourists had not returned. How much longer would we have?

"Don't be afraid," he said. "God is in control. He didn't provide us with this miracle for us to be caught at the last minute, so close to our goal."

I watched as he crawled over the bags and slid into the front seat. He opened the door and I grimaced as the dome light came on. He quickly shut the door and the light went out. Momentarily, the back door opened. He pulled out the over-stuffed plastic bags one at a time until enough were piled on the ground to give us maneuvering room. I was able to wriggle the rest of the Bibles from their hiding places.

As soon as the last one was out, I helped Lon arrange the plastic bags, one on top of the other, until all of them were back inside the van. They filled the entire space from floor to ceiling. Just at that moment, we heard people laughing. The tourists were returning.

We closed the back door as quietly as we could, hastened to the front doors and got in. We slithered on top of the bags in the back, closed the curtain, and held our breath. Within minutes, we heard the snort and rumble of the tour bus as its engine came to life. Light filtered through above the curtains when the bus driver turned on the headlights. I could see Lon's face. He didn't look scared. He looked determined.

We watched through the curtain slits as the bus drove away. The blue neon sign over the restaurant suddenly went dark. After a half hour, all the rest of the people in the restaurant got into their cars and drove away. The vacant lot was truly vacant, except for us. We were completely alone, lying on top of God's promised books.

We moved to the front seats of the van and did our best to sleep, sitting upright in our seats. God had been faithful, providing us with an amazing miracle, and we felt his protection as we dozed throughout the night.

We woke with a start at the sound of a car horn. We looked at each other, then out the window. It was already morning. Surprisingly, the *Casa Escu* was open for business and a few cars were already parked near us.

"Time to get out of here," Lon said. He started the engine and we drove away, our precious contraband behind us in plastic bags piled clear up to the ceiling.

# CHAPTER 14

# Transfer

We drove around Bucharest for some time, but every black Dak sedan that sped by made us nervous. We left Bucharest with the hope of spending the day out of the view of the Securitate. We felt conspicuous. We were well aware of how dangerous it was for us to be pulled over.

It was late morning before we realized we had made an error. When we removed the Bibles from the hidden recesses of the van, we had forgotten to take out any food from the little refrigerator, which was now buried beneath bags and bags of Bibles. All the canned goods were under the benches, so also out of reach. By noon, we were hungry, not having eaten since mid-afternoon the previous day. We praised God when we saw a farmer's roadside stand. We pulled over immediately.

We bought a large loaf of dense, crunchy bread and some cheese from the skinny, old farmer. As with most Romanians, it was difficult to tell how old he was. The people were poor, hardworking, with little medical or dental care and not enough to eat. He nodded and grinned a toothless smile as we selected our not-so-favorite beverage, *CeCe*, which was all he had in the way of bottled drinks.

As we paid for our purchases, we saw a man leaning against the farm stand, eating a large green pepper as if it were an apple. We wanted something other than bread and cheese, so we added several green peppers to our purchases. When we bit into one, it was juicy and delicious—probably the best green pepper I had ever eaten.

With our purchases in our arms, we walked away from the road to a large tree, which provided good shade and cover. We sat underneath its broad, leafy arms to enjoy our lunch. We tore off hunks of bread, added the smelly but delicious cheese, and savored every bite. The peppers slaked our thirst, and the *CeCe* served as our dessert.

Everything was so peaceful and serene. Our ragged nerves were eventually soothed, and we began to breathe easier. Birds sang above in the tree, a soft breeze blew through our hair, and the sun warmed our clothes. With our backs against the trunk, sitting side-by-side, we held hands and fell into a peaceful sleep—the first restful sleep in days.

We awoke with a start and the first thing we did was look for the camper van, thankful that it was where we had parked it, undisturbed. We scrambled up and dusted breadcrumbs from our laps. I yawned and stretched my arms. I felt completely refreshed, and by the smile Lon gave me, I could tell he felt equally renewed.

The old farmer saw us and gave a friendly wave. What he must have thought of us sleeping under his tree for hours. We climbed back into the van and drove back to Bucharest. It was already four o'clock. We still had a couple of hours before our rendezvous. We drove deep into the city and found our way to the other side. We parked, resting our eyes.

"It is almost over," Lon said. "The Lord is with us."

"And with the underground church in Romania. Let's go."

We drove back to the Opera Nationala and followed the route that Teodor laid out for us. We arrived miraculously at the base of the hill with the white stone church at the top. We pulled up behind a little white Dak and turned off the engine. We were relieved to see Nadia and Elika get out of the car and go for a stroll. They were both wearing sweaters over their dresses. They didn't even glance at our van as they passed.

I had to force myself to breathe. Lon kept his eye on the side mirror as I watched the road ahead. There appeared to be nothing out of the usual, but that didn't really mean anything. The Securitate had a way of signaling ahead and staking out whole areas with informers. If we were under suspicion, it wouldn't be long before they would surround us, arrest Nadia and Elika, and figure out what to do with the Americans. I prayed under my breath the whole time.

I glanced at my side mirror when I saw movement. Nadia and Elika were returning. Nadia was whistling and her sweater was over her arm. Elika had her arm around the waist of her friend, and they looked like two good friends out for a stroll. They got back into the car. As Elika started the car, Lon started the van. As they pulled out, we started to pull out. Suddenly, a red car came out of nowhere and pulled up right behind Elika's Dak as it entered the street. There was nothing we could do. We pulled out into the street behind the red car.

"Oh, God," Lon said in a whisper.

"What should we do?"

"Keep following. There might not be anything to it."

We kept our eyes on the white Dak in front of the red car. Elika drove down the hill and then turned left. The red car turned left. We turned left. Elika drove through several streets, the red car behind her the whole way. We followed both cars.

"What are we going to do?" I asked. "This looks really suspicious."

"I don't know. Let's keep going. If we don't do it now, how will we get rid of these Bibles?"

"Lord Jesus, help us! Send that red car away!" I prayed desperately out loud.

As soon as I spoke my prayer, the red car turned off onto another road and disappeared. We looked at each other, burst out laughing, and thanked God profusely for His protection. We were now directly behind the white Dak.

The sudden arrival of that red car must have been equally unnerving to Elika. She continued to wind her vehicle through the streets on the outskirts of Bucharest for another hour. Eventually, she drove onto a main road and appeared to be going directly north.

The sun began to set and shafts of orange and red light flickered through the van illuminating the sharp edges of tall buildings, bridges and construction equipment. As we left the city, the sun disappeared, darkness descended and we turned on our headlights. The road ahead was straight and paved.

We traveled behind Elika's car for another hour, keeping our eyes glued to her taillights. I could see tall trees on either side of the road. Suddenly, without warning, the Dak veered to the side of the road and stopped. Lon pulled the van up behind and shut off the engine and headlights.

Elika and Nadia jumped out of the car. We joined the women on the empty road. It was pitch dark. Nadia held a flashlight and began sweeping the beam across a dense forest. I could see the trunks of tall pines but little else.

Within seconds, a number of men ran out of the darkness. Several rushed the van and flung open the back doors. They quickly formed a human chain, pulling the bags from the back and passing them down the line. Lon and I stood dumbfounded as the garbage bags filled with Bibles, songbooks and printer's ink passed from one to another until they disappeared in the darkness. It was all over in minutes.

The men nearest us breathlessly shook our hands, spoke their quick appreciation, ran into the forest after their companions and were gone. Elika gave us a quick hug and ran back to her car. She started the engine and drove away, leaving us behind. We stood alone on the road, watching the red taillights fade into the distance.

"God bless you."

We jumped at Nadia's voice. We didn't know she was still there.

"Remember me," she said in hushed tones. "Nadia Constantinescu."

She grabbed my hands and pulled me into her. Her eyes, swimming with tears, stared into mine. I knew this would be the last time I would see her. Part of me longed to extend the moment and I knew she felt the same. I took particular notice of her face: narrow and pale, glowing and flattened in the moonless night, heavy eyebrows, small thin lips—and beautiful blue eyes brimming with love and gratitude.

"I will," I said, choking on emotion. I was deeply aware of this singular moment. "I promise, Nadia. God bless… "

She hugged me, spun on her heels, ran into the forest and vanished in the night. Lon and I stood in complete darkness, alone on the road beside our empty smuggler's van. Squeezing each other's hand, we struggled to absorb the magnitude of what had occurred.

Our mission was accomplished. The five thousand Bibles, twenty-five hundred songbooks, and cans of printer's ink were now in the hands of Romania's underground church.

"Wow!" Lon said, breaking the silence that had enveloped us.

"Yeah, wow," I echoed. "We did it."

"God did it."

"Yes. God did it. We are just his couriers."

Lon whistled low. The sound barely reached my ears. I strained to hear his voice as he spoke almost to himself. "It's more. More than we can comprehend. They prayed for a few Bibles and God gave them thousands. They would have been happy with five and we brought five thousand. I'm just now getting it. We limit God, you know? We ask for so little and expect less, and then he gives…"

"Abundantly. Everything… perfect. Perfect."

"Let's thank Him."

"Lord, we thank you and praise you!" I prayed out loud. The sound carried in the empty darkness, so I lowered my voice and gave Lon's hand a squeeze. "Continue to protect those Bibles and the people who hold them in their hands. Let them be like a mighty sword to cut through the chains of Communism and free the Romanians. Use those Bibles, our great and loving God. Use these Bibles to set them free!"

Lon put his arm around my shoulder as we gazed out at the trees where the Bibles, the men, and our contact Nadia had disappeared. "And protect us now, Lord, as we return to our home and our children," he said quietly, squeezing my shoulder. "Keep us safe on the road and be with us as we cross the borders. Amen."

We stepped back into the van and took advantage of the deserted road to return things to order, replacing the side panels and locking them into place. We transferred our recent purchases from beneath my side of the front seat to the back. We stayed on the side of the road, trying to determine what we should do next. I pulled out some of the tourist pamphlets from the glove box.

"How about going to the Black Sea," I said, unfolding a brochure. "It's a well-known tourist attraction. It's supposed to have incredible mud baths. Lots of Eastern Europeans go there for their vacation."

"You mean where Party officials go? You want to leave a custom-made smuggler's van with Dutch plates in the midst of them?"

"But when are we ever going to be this close to the Black Sea?" I argued. "We could wallow like pigs in their famous mud. We need to relax. God won't mind."

"Or we could drive into Yugoslavia and head south to the Adriatic," Lon countered. "They call it the Riviera of the East. Can you see yourself sunbathing on the beach?"

"That sounds better than mud. How long will that take?" I said, putting the brochures back into the glove box.

"Another day's drive at least. I want to get out of Romania as soon as possible. We don't want to overstay our welcome."

"I see what you mean. Part of me wants to stay because the people we've met here have been so good to us, but I know we won't see them again," I said. "I will never forget Nadia or Elika."

"Or Teodor or Elisabet."

We stared into the night, thinking of the wonderful Christians we had met. "Let's go to the Adriatic," I said. "We deserve it, don't you think?"

"Of course, we do, darling," he said, patting my hand.

"But I miss the boys terribly," I said, feeling an all too familiar maternal pull in my gut.

Lon smiled at me indulgently. "Me, too. You want to go directly home then?"

"Kind of. I don't know. When are we ever going to be this close to the Adriatic Riviera?"

"That's true. Why don't we wait until we cross into Yugoslavia and then decide."

"Sounds good to me," I said.

He turned the key, made a three-point turn, and drove for an hour before we saw the streetlights of Bucharest. The two-lane road was devoid of cars. We discussed the fact that we were probably violating a mandatory curfew, but didn't care. We felt invisible, invincible, and inviolable. God was on our side.

# CHAPTER 15

# Bad Gas

The city was empty as we drove silently back into Bucharest. Curfew was in effect and very few vehicles were on the road. We easily found our way to the main highway that would take us westward through the city.

Once we were on the other side, we decided to turn north, following the signs to Pitesti, one of the larger cities in Romania. From there we would go west and then head south toward the Romanian/ Yugoslavian border.

Now that our mission was complete, we couldn't wait to leave Romania. We were not out of the woods yet. Even though the contraband was gone, our smuggler's van posed an even greater risk to us if we were caught. Since we could no longer prove we had smuggled Bibles, Romanian officials could easily deduce that we had smuggled drugs or weapons. Who was to say? The penalty for smuggling guns and drugs was death. I didn't know the penalty for smuggling Bibles. At the very least, it would mean imprisonment. The sooner we crossed the Romanian border and entered Yugoslavia, the better.

Since we'd had a good sleep that afternoon, we decided not to stop and headed quickly to the border. We left Bucharest behind and turned north toward Pitesti, where we hoped to pick up the main southern route.

Without a map, we relied entirely on highway signs. We found that this sometimes took us further afield than if we had a map to guide us. Fortunately, my husband was gifted with a sense of direction. After traveling a long distance that day, we realized that our gas gauge was nearing empty. We needed to fill up.

To our dismay, all the gas stations we passed were closed. Romania was not like America with a gas station on every corner. The chances of finding a twenty-four hour station were zilch.

Even more distressing, we needed a gas station that dispensed diesel fuel. In our haste to leave Bucharest, we had forgotten that diesel stations were only available near the cities, and only open during the day.

We anxiously scanned the dark highway for the blue sign of an official campground. Without a map, we had no idea where to go. There was nothing we could do. We had to wait for morning.

We pulled off the road and drove into a culvert behind some tall bushes, which hid us from view. It was the best we could do in the dark. We pulled the bench out and laid the mattress down. We curled up together and talked quietly about the miracles from the past few days. Eventually, sleep overcame us and we relived our experiences in our dreams.

Morning came and we drove to Pitesti where we filled up the tank. We drove for four more hours to Sebeş and then west across southern Transylvania to Arad. The drive was very enjoyable. We felt light-hearted and stopped often to take photographs of the scenery.

We passed many gypsy camps along the way. The Roma had been as persecuted as the Jews and the Christians during World War II, and it was good to see them with their horse-drawn caravans. Their canvas-covered carts sat on wooden wheels or narrow rubber tires. The gypsies sat near campfires waiting for dinner or lay resting under the shade of their carts.

At Arad, we turned due south toward Timisoara, a city built on the site of an ancient Roman fortress. As the largest city in western Romania, it was a commercial and manufacturing hub influenced by many cultures. We did not go into the downtown area although it would have been a great tourist destination. We kept going, hoping to cross the border in daylight.

As we left the city behind, the beautiful onion-shaped spires on the top of the Eastern Orthodox churches gave us hope for a new day in Romania. We drove for another hour before we stopped at the side of the road to fix lunch. We had about another half hour before we reached the border of Yugoslavia.

"We're almost there," I said. "So far, so good. We're going to breeze through the border, I can just feel it." Lon didn't reply. His silence spoke volumes. "Hey, what's wrong?"

"I've made a mistake," he said, rubbing his forehead. "We should have filled up in Timisoara. We're running low on gas."

"Surely there will be one before we come to the border."

"There better be or we'll be in trouble. Keep your eyes peeled."

We passed through one small village after another but didn't see any gas stations. We were now running on our reserve tank. We were only a few miles from the border when we drove through a small village.

"There," I shouted.

I had seen a gas pump set back off the road among the trees. Lon turned the van around and drove down the dirt road to the gas station. We pulled up to two old-fashioned fuel pumps. They had once been white but were now covered with rust.

We weren't even sure they were operable. A young man sauntered out of a shack and came to see the camper van. We asked for gas, but he didn't acknowledge us. He walked around the vehicle and lovingly touched its sides.

"Diesel?" Lon asked.

He pointed to the pump on the right, afterward ignoring us. He had eyes only for our shiny blue camper van.

We filled up and paid him, using the last of our leu. It didn't matter. We were within a few kilometers of the border and would exchange our money into Yugoslavian dinar.

As we approached the border, I began to pray. In my heart, I knew that God was with us, but I was still anxious about crossing into Yugoslavia. After waiting in line for only a half-hour, we pulled up to the gate and greeted the dour-faced border guards.

We handed over our passports and waited. There was some confusion and conversation among the guards about our passports— oddly they didn't have the requisite stamp for entering Romania. I began praying very hard. The guards, appearing embarrassed by the oversight, stamped both our passports. The red and white crossing bar rose and they waved us through.

As I looked through the back windows at the lowering crossing bar, my spirit lifted. I felt lighter than I had in days. It was as if I had been holding my breath the whole time. We praised God that we had successfully completed our mission in Romania and had made it out alive. We drove directly south toward Belgrade. We were on our way.

Ten miles later, a terrible sound came from the engine.

"Did you hear that?" Lon asked.

"What was it?" I asked.

"I don't know."

Almost immediately, we heard a *clank*, a *clunk* and an ear-piercing *screech* of grinding metal as the engine seized. We were barely able to pull over to the side of the road. The engine was dead. Lon tried to turn it over, but we only heard the click of the ignition. We got out, and opened the hood. Pungent black smoke poured out of the engine.

"This is bad, isn't it?" I said, waving my hand as the smoke curled into the air. "What on earth happened?"

"I'm afraid I know."

"What? What is it?"

"Bad gas. That last gas station in Romania. I don't think that pump was diesel."

"What does that mean?"

"It means the engine is destroyed."

"Destroyed!" The news horrified me. "It can't be! What are we going to do?"

"I guess what we did when we first met. Remember?" Lon gave me a sheepish grin.

"I'm not following. What did we do?"

"Hitchhike."

"Here? Are you kidding? Where?"

"That way," he said and waved to the right, as he peered at the engine. "Towards Belgrade."

"And leave the van?" Panic began to take over.

"I'm sorry, honey. We haven't got a choice. I'm not leaving you here alone, and we can't just sit here. You remember what Open Doors said? We're on our own. Come on. Don't worry. It will be okay. God is with us. Do you want to pray?"

"Yes. We need to pray, " I said, grabbing his hands in mine. "Lord, we need your help right now. You've been with us through this whole trip. We trust you to show us the way. Amen."

We hugged and then went to the road's edge. It was completely vacant in both directions. On either side were flat fields, not a house in sight. The horizon was void of trees or buildings. We waited for thirty minutes without seeing any cars. It was hot outside, not even a slight breeze to cool us off. I was getting sunburned so went back to sit in the van. I watched as Lon stood at the side of the road, looking one way and then the other.

We saw them at the same time. Several cars were coming our way at a high rate of speed. Lon stepped to the side of the road and began waving his arm. The first car whizzed by. The second car passed and then suddenly braked, pulling to the side. Behind it, following too close, a third car plowed into the second car. A fourth car swerved, nearly hitting a truck coming the other way, and sped on to the sound of blaring horns.

Meanwhile, the drivers of the two cars on the side of the road in front of us got out and began yelling at each other. We stood helplessly by as our good Samaritan defended his actions, gesticulating toward us. The other driver didn't care. He pointed to his damaged car, shouting and cursing.

As the two drivers examined the dents, yelling at the top of their lungs, we debated whether we should get involved. When the two squared off, fists raised, we decided against it and went back to wait in the van. We took the opportunity to pray once more.

Before long, our hearts sank further as we heard the terrifying *dee dow, dee dow, dee dow* of a siren and saw the flashing blue lights of a police car. I wanted to shrink Lon, the van, and me to the size of a mouse as the police car pulled over behind the two cars.

A tall officer, dressed in a khaki uniform, got out of his small police car and walked up to the angry drivers. They both stopped yelling and calmed down as he approached and spoke to them. We gulped as we saw them point to our van, the real cause of the collision.

"He's going to come over here," I whispered.

"I expect so," Lon replied in a strained voice. "Keep praying."

"What are we going to say?"

"Remember that verse the Lord gave us before?"

"Yes. I memorized it. When you are brought before them, do not worry about how you will defend yourselves or what you will say, for the Holy Spirit will teach you at that time what you should say."

"That's the one. I think this is why. We prayed. We know God hears us. Let's trust the Lord. He will see us through. It's all going to work out for our good. You'll see. At least, I hope so. I never anticipated this happening."

At that moment, the Yugoslavian policeman started toward us. We both got out of the van as he approached. He was handsome, lean and only a few years older than us.

"Is everyone all right?" Lon asked loudly.

His English words stopped the officer in his tracks. After recovering from his shock, he advanced.

"You are English," the policeman said in English.

"Americans, sir."

"Passports, please."

We handed our passports to him. His face was immobile as he thumbed through the pages. I saw his eyebrows rise as he noticed we had just come from Romania. He handed them back to us.

"What is the problem?" he asked, looking at the van.

"Bad gas, Lon answered. "The engine is… *kaput*."

"*Yah?*" The policeman opened the hood and looked at the engine, tinkering with the cables, etc. until satisfied. "You try key?"

Lon got into the van and tried the ignition. It was the same as before. No go. He got back out and stood beside the policeman as they both stared at the engine as if that could fix it. I stood silently, praying under my breath.

"We're sorry if we caused this accident."

"You? No. They go too fast. I follow them. One moment."

He walked back to the two drivers, wrote them both a ticket and made them move their cars. Just as they pulled back onto the road, another car sped by and swerved to miss them. The two cars pulled back off the road and stopped.

The policeman ran to his car, jumped in and drove after the speeding car, his lights flashing and siren blaring. The drivers of the other two vehicles pulled back onto the road and followed at a much-reduced speed.

Lon and I looked at each other and shrugged. It was all so surreal. We were again alone on the side of the two-lane, deserted road. The sun was blazing. The road radiated heat. I felt sweat trickle down my back. A dust devil spun up the road sending dust particles into our faces. We ran back to the van and got in.

"What now?" I asked, wiping my sweaty face with a paper towel. I tried to sound cheerful but failed miserably.

"I don't know. I'm afraid to try hitchhiking again. Can you believe what happened? At least no one got hurt."

"That policeman was nice," I said, trying to be hopeful.

"How 'bout that he spoke English. What are the odds?"

"I don't care. What are we going to do now, Lon? It's too hot to walk. We can't hitchhike. We don't speak the language. The policeman left us. We're stuck."

"I don't know, honey. I honestly don't have a clue," he said. "Let's have lunch. Maybe it will help me think. I just don't know what we're going to do. I can't believe this happened. We were so close."

I was startled by the tone of his voice. I looked closely. I could tell by his face that he was downcast. My usually upbeat husband was worried. He never failed to lift my spirit, but now his spirit needed lifting. I felt guilty for adding to his burden by my whining and lack of faith.

After everything we'd been through, every disappointment or challenge we'd faced, he had always kept faith and a positive outlook. We had overcome so much on this trip and had seen miracle after miracle, yet in this moment we felt overwhelmed and helpless. The demise of the van was a big blow. I had never seen him so low.

We spent the next few minutes preparing lunch. I chattered like a magpie, saying anything that popped into my head, trying to lift the somber mood. A few times, he looked up and smiled. It encouraged me so I kept talking, relying on familiar and funny stories from our time in Holland.

I heated some soup on the stove and he set up the little table. We had some bread from the previous day, so we ate it with our soup. We were just finishing when we heard a knock on the rear doors. My stomach clenched and I held my breath. Lon opened the doors.

The young policeman stood before us with a big grin on his face.

"So this is where you are. You show me?"

What could we do? We welcomed him into the van, our hearts in our throats, and showed him the various features of our camper van. He was very curious and highly impressed. He thanked us for the demonstration of the stove, refrigerator, and bed, and then we followed him out, shutting the rear doors.

"I have truck come to take this to Beograd [Belgrade]. I drive you there. You come with me. They will bring later." He seemed very pleased with himself, but we were visibly upset. "What is wrong?"

What were we to say? I took a deep breath and asked God to give me the words and speak through me.

"We are so thankful for your help, sir, but I have all my things in here. I don't want to leave them. Someone might … I have many… presents, gifts… for my children. It is a very new van. People will be curious. Can we not wait until the truck comes?"

He followed my words closely. He pushed his hat back on his head and smiled his understanding. "I will see when truck comes," he smiled. "Then I practice English while we wait." He walked back to his patrol car. We breathed a sigh of relief.

It took an hour for the tow truck to arrive. While we waited, we sat in the van and conversed with Officer Miroslav, who had only recently graduated from the police academy. He was a charming person. He taught us a few words in his native language and was eager to speak English. He asked many questions about American culture. The way he spoke to us, I felt like a celebrity.

He had heard many stories about America, some of them outrageous—everybody was rich, every room in every house had a television, police were actually given patrol cars and weapons and did not have to buy them for themselves. I couldn't say that everything he said was wrong, but I was uncomfortable with the way Americans were portrayed as rich and our lives without strife.

As a young military family, we could barely pay for our rent, food, car payments, and insurance. What we had that they didn't have— the one thing no one here spoke about—was our freedom. We were free to speak our minds, free to be individuals, free to travel, free to practice our faith.

Although Tito's Yugoslavia was fairly liberal by Communist standards, there was no tolerance for those who wanted another way. Dissenters, even Christians, were considered terrorists and anarchists, and were not to be trusted. Many were punished severely if caught. The jails were filled with priests and pastors.

Officer Miroslav peppered us with questions from the simple to the more difficult. We didn't know if he was interrogating us or satisfying a deep hunger to know about America. We answered simply, mostly yes and no, hoping to cut off his inquiry, but the questions kept coming.

What was our favorite food? What countries did we visit? Did we have more than one car? How could we afford such a beautiful vehicle and be so young? What did we do for fun? What was our president like? Did we know Mick Jagger? Did we know Rock

Hudson? Did we live with our parents? What music did we like? What was Romania like? What did we do in Romania?

He was eager to know everything—his youthful exuberance was infectious—as if this unexpected and rare time with two Americans was the answer to his yearning. To turn him away from his inquiries into our time in Romania, we diverted him with questions about his own life. Did he have brothers and sisters? What kind of schooling did he have? What should we eat in Yugoslavia?

There was a moment in our friendly conversation when I forgot that we were talking to a Yugoslavian policeman who was sitting on a bench that had recently hidden over a million dollars worth of contraband.

# CHAPTER 16

# The Ford Motor Plant

I sat in the back and Lon sat in front of Officer Miroslav's police car as we followed the tow truck to Belgrade. The young officer was still talking, still asking us questions. I guess he knew that he only had so much time to practice his English. He was like a sponge, soaking up everything he could learn from us. We tried to be as open and honest as possible with our answers, conscious of the fact we held a dangerous secret.

We arrived at the Ford plant in Officer Miroslav's police car, which made an impression on the employees because he had turned on his blue flashing lights. It was a huge building with a tower of twenty or more stories in the center and large, squat buildings of four stories on either side. We watched as the tow truck took our van down a slope and disappeared into one of several repair bays below ground.

Officer Miroslav stopped his car, turned off the lights and escorted us into the front office on the ground floor of the tower. As we entered, he spoke to the receptionist. She nodded and picked up the phone. He gestured for us to sit in chairs that were against the wall. He sat next to us.

"Your van go now to repair. They take good care of you. I have their… attention," he said and smiled broadly. "Thank you for telling me about America. I have enjoyed so much to meet you. I hope all is good for you."

"It was our pleasure, Officer Miroslav. Thank you for all your help. We will remember your kindness and always be grateful." Lon shook his hand. I gave him a quick hug, and impulsively whispered, "Bless you."

He tipped his hat, and we waved goodbye as he left. Although we were at an American-owned company, we were well aware that our van, equipped for smuggling, was now in the hands of Yugoslav workers who would have complete access to it. What if they discovered the hidden compartments?

There was nothing we could do but trust in the Lord. We took a seat in the waiting room and spent the time silently praying. We asked God to cover the workers' sight and confuse them so that no one would find the hidden latch or notice the now-hollow sound of the empty side panels.

"Excuse me. You come with me?"

We looked up into the face of the young receptionist. She wore a solid gray suit with sturdy black pumps. Her long dark hair was pulled back into a ponytail. She seemed very grim. My stomach did a flip-flop. We'd been waiting about an hour, plenty of time for them to discover that our van was no ordinary Ford van.

"What is it?" Lon asked as we stood. "Have you found the problem?"

She shook her head. "Please, come. Now, please."

We stood our ground. I grabbed Lon's hand. "Where are we going?"

"Please," she urged, taking my arm and drawing me toward the door. "Come."

I looked back at Lon. He shrugged, and we followed her out the door, down a hallway, and to an elevator. She punched the button, the door opened and she ushered us in. We were surprised when she inserted a key in the panel, turned it, and a button at the top of the panel lit up. She stepped out of the elevator, turned and walked away. The doors closed and we headed upward alone.

When the doors opened, a man in a navy blue business suit welcomed us. He was of middle height, muscularly built, tending toward flab. He was clean-shaven, with a round face and large nose. He grabbed our hands and pumped them.

"Welcome, my American friends. I am Darko Petranovic. I am the director. This is my company. Please to come in. Here, sit here," he said, sweeping his arm to an area with a couch, coffee table and overstuffed chairs.

Bewildered, we followed him into his penthouse. I glanced around and saw a dining area by a glass wall that overlooked the city of Belgrade. I could also see a full kitchen and several rooms beyond the living area. We sat together on the couch. He pulled one of the large chairs closer to us and sat down.

"Have you eaten? I have arranged for a lunch. That is good, yes?"

We were dumbfounded. We were expecting to be interrogated about our smuggling operation, and here we were being offered lunch by the head of the Ford Motor plant in Belgrade, Yugoslavia.

"Yes. That is good," was all we managed to say. He nodded his happy approval, picked up the phone and spoke something unintelligible to us.

"So! You are Americans!"

"Yes."

"You are traveling in our country?"

"Yes. We are tourists. It is our first time here."

"How you like our country?"

"We love it. It is very beautiful," I said enthusiastically. His happy face made me want to please him.

"*Da*! True. What have you seen?"

Was this a trick? Was this his way of gaining our confidence and making us slip up? Lon told him where we had traveled, what we had seen, what we liked and what we had eaten.

He seemed very pleased with our answers, beaming with pleasure. We were cautious, but his enthusiasm was infectious. He appeared to want us to like him and his country.

"But what are you doing here? Why have you come to my country?"

I didn't know what to say. My mind spun with possible answers, but Lon didn't miss a beat.

"We were visiting Austria and heard from many people that Yugoslavia is even more beautiful. We had to see for ourselves."

Mr. Petranovic was immensely pleased and responded to what Lon said by giving his own commentary on what we had seen and the towns we had travelled through. He was eager to show how modern Yugoslavia had become, how proud he was of it.

When the elevator opened again, he jumped up. He greeted a man who pushed a cart into the room. It was filled with serving dishes and plates. Everything smelled wonderful.

He dismissed the man and pushed the cart over to the couch. He took great delight in serving us and placing the dishes in front of us on the coffee table. Our china plates were filled with sliced potatoes, an assortment of cold meats, marinated vegetables and pureed carrots.

He handed us fine linen napkins. We unfolded them, placed them on our laps, took our plates and ate. We made the appropriate sounds of appreciation, which made him smile all the more. I was very hungry and the wonderful flavors eased my nervousness.

While we ate, he asked us questions about America. Similar to Officer Miroslav's impressions, Mr. Petranovic had a grandiose view of American life, but it was soon obvious that his appreciation was more sophisticated.

I finished my meal as the conversation moved to his favorite subject: cars. Lon and he spoke about the cars they had owned and what cars were now available in America, their features, engines, and so forth. This left me to gaze in quiet wonder at the opulence of the room and the view of the city below.

Mr. Petranovic was extremely interested with what was happening in the American car market. He asked Lon about how the Pinto was selling and whether GMC's Gremlin would be competition. He asked about the new Ford F-150 pickup truck. It was obvious that he knew more than we did about Ford's operations in America.

As soon as I set my empty plate on the table, he jumped up and cleared the dishes. From underneath the top tray, he pulled out demitasse cups on saucers and set them before us. Then he removed a small silver pot and poured a black liquid into them. As he did so, he explained the history and the process of making perfect Turkish coffee.

Its consistency was almost syrupy, and it was strong. He saw my expression when I tasted it and apologized for not offering me sugar and milk. He tried to hide his disappointment as I "doctored" my coffee. I ladled in two scoops of brown crystals from the sugar bowl and as much milk as I could fit in the small cup. It was much more palatable and I could feel the caffeine coursing through my system. He watched my every move and I was more than a little self-conscious. I savored the strong coffee because it was really good. I smiled at him.

"It is the best coffee I've ever had," I said, meaning every word. He leaned back in his chair and sighed. I was relieved that I had made him so happy.

"Now," he said, "let us see what is happening to your vehicle."

He picked up the phone and made the call. He listened and I could see his pleasant face change to concern. Uh-oh, here it comes, I thought. The party is over. They've discovered our secret. They were Ford technicians. They would know that our Ford van was altered to serve as a smuggler's van.

He hung up, and then dialed another number. He spoke for some time. The palms of my hands began to sweat and I again began to pray. We had come so far unscathed. Were we now going to have to answer for what we did? I looked at my husband. He appeared completely at ease. He winked at me.

Mr. Petranovic hung up and looked at us gravely. Seeing my worried face, he managed to smile. "It is not good news. I am sorry. There is much damage to the engine. It is broken, *kaput*. This vehicle, it requires special fuel. It is too bad that you filled it with regular fuel." He looked at us like a stern schoolmaster.

"I was afraid of that," Lon said. "The man at the gas station said it was diesel, but I had my doubts. It was a very small gas station. It only had two old, rusty pumps."

"Where was this?" he asked.

I held my breath, wondering what Lon would say.

"Romania."

"*Ne*! Romania! They are all liars! They will sell their own mothers. That is a very bad country. Very bad. Why would you go there?"

"We wanted to see Bucharest and the Black Sea. But, I agree, it is not a good country. Not like here."

"It's true! The Socialist Republic of Yugoslavia is a great country. I am so happy that you agree."

"We completely agree," I said. "We love it here, but we are eager to get home. We have children waiting for us. Two little boys."

His face changed from excitement to grimness.

"Can you fix it?" Lon asked.

He brightened, "Yes. Yes. We fix. But we do not have the part we need. We must send for a new part for you. Tomorrow or the next day, we fix it."

"Oh dear," I said. "Well, thank you for being so kind. We won't take any more of your time."

"Yes, thank you," Lon said as we both rose. "You've been a wonderful host and we will tell all our American friends what a great country Yugoslavia is and how kind the people are. Thank you, Mr. Petranovic. We need to find a place to stay for the night. Can you suggest some place we might stay?"

"*Ne, ne*. I have arranged everything! You will stay at Hotel Beograd. My gift to you. I have called for a taxi to take you there. You don't worry about anything. We fix it. You see."

He would accept nothing less than our agreement to take him up on his offer. We were overwhelmed by his generosity. We shook his hand and said goodbye as the elevator doors opened. He waved to us as the doors closed and we descended.

When the elevator doors opened on the first floor, the receptionist was waiting for us and escorted us to a taxi. Our suitcases were already stored in the trunk and before long we were whisked to the luxurious Hotel Beograd overlooking the shores of the beautiful Danube River.

Once in our rooms, we put a call through to Brother Andrew's Open Doors. We explained our situation and asked them what they wanted us to do. They prayed about it and felt no peace about leaving the van in the care of the Ford Motor plant in Yugoslavia. They were as concerned as we were that the alterations to the van would be discovered.

After much discussion, it was decided that we would not wait for the engine part to arrive, but have the van towed to a secure lot. Open Doors would immediately send a tow truck to remove the van and take it back to Holland, a matter of two days.

We were instructed to take the next available train out of the country. Since our mission was complete, they did not want us in any more danger. We felt bad about putting them to so much trouble and expense, but there was nothing we could do. The chance that the smuggling alterations would be discovered increased with every minute the van was at the Ford Motor plant.

With the help of the concierge, who thankfully spoke English, we were able to locate a secure parking lot. He helped us contact the Ford plant and explained that we decided not to wait for the part and wanted the van to be moved. Surprisingly, everything went as we hoped. Within an hour, the van was moved into a secure lot and our greatest fear was put to rest.

We returned to the hotel and spent an incredible evening of leisure sitting in the restaurant lounge, eating appetizers and watching the lights of the boats glittering on the Danube before returning to our luxurious room where we immediately fell asleep on down-covered beds.

The next morning we took a taxi to the secure lot, pulled the rest of our bags and souvenirs out, double checked to make sure nothing had been disturbed, and laid our hands on the van and prayed for its protection.

The taxi driver must have thought we had lost our minds, seeing us putting our hands on the hood, the sides, the rear doors, and the roof, but we risked his mocking us to assure its safety. We waited for the security guard to lock the gate and then we went to the train station.

It was time for us to leave.

# CHAPTER 17

# Refugees on a Train

The train station was located in the center of the city. Even though this was the capital city of Yugoslavia, its international train station was small, dirty, smelly, and stifling hot.

There were so many people in the building we had to push our way to the ticket counter. We purchased two tickets to Holland. We would travel to Zagreb to Ljubljana, Austria, and then on to Munich, where we would change trains to Holland. We maneuvered our way through a thick crowd to the platform outside. It was no better. In fact, it was worse.

The temperature was close to eighty degrees and the smell of unwashed bodies filled the air. The concrete platform was narrow and filled with hundreds of people, most of whom were carrying cloth bundles, boxes tied with twine, and straw baskets rather than suitcases. I felt like I'd stepped onto the film stage of a movie about refugees fleeing a war in a Third World country.

We watched as a train pulled up and the people raced to jump onto it. The train was old with peeling, dark olive paint and rust along the sides. Our eyes widened as men scrambled up onto the roof of the train, friends tossing their bundles up to them. They held on for dear life as the train chugged out of sight.

Our train was due in fifteen minutes, but it was more than an hour before it arrived. We were just beginning to think we had missed it as we sat listlessly on our suitcases. We felt a shift in the crowd and saw people craning their necks to see down the tracks.

As the train slowed to a stop, we were jostled and bumped as passengers surged forward to get on. Lon saw immediately that we needed to move quickly or be left behind. He elbowed his way through, dragging me along by one hand.

I gripped the handle of my suitcase, fearing it would be torn from my hands as people banged into it, jumped over it or pushed it out of their way. With Lon pulling on my hand and my suitcase knocked and buffeted about I was almost torn in two.

With inhuman effort, Lon and I lunged onto the train steps, dragging our luggage behind us. Lon turned to the left and we clambered past people, looking for a place to sit. By the grace of God we found an empty compartment with nice, cushioned benches on both sides. We placed our suitcases and souvenirs in the overhead bin and sat down near the door.

An old woman, her grandchildren, and three men soon joined us in the small compartment. There was much jostling and organizing before the grandmother situated her three grandchildren at her sides and arranged a large straw-covered basket at her feet. The men sat next to me, pressing me into Lon. We were packed in like canned sardines.

We decided to get the introductions over before the train started. The children were excited to be sitting with two Americans. The oldest girl, Valinka, who was twelve, spoke a little English and shyly explained that they were going to Munich to stay with their father. Their grandmother would be returning to Romania after seeing them safely in Munich. She introduced her eight-year-old sister and her brother, who was seven. The little ones stared at us with awe and hid their faces when I said hello to them.

The man next to me introduced himself as Juergen Brunner, a Swiss student, who had been backpacking through Yugoslavia. Unfortunately, he only spoke German and my German was only good for planning covert operations.

Next to him was Buklev Bronkovic, a physics teacher. He spoke excellent English and surprised us by saying this was his first time speaking our language. He had learned the language from a record and was eager to try his skill. He was traveling with a colleague, Juraj Kurcovic, to a conference in Austria. We were grateful we had such nice people sharing our compartment as the train began filling up with more people.

By the time the train began to move, there was absolutely no more room and the air was horribly hot and stinky. The pathway between compartments was completely filled with men, women, and children sitting on the floor. We could hear footsteps above us as latecomers took precarious seats on the roof of the train.

All was well during the first two hours as we traveled toward the Austrian border. We spoke cautiously to Buklev who asked us many questions. We didn't want to be rude or suspicious, but we were not out of the woods here yet. There was every chance that this "lucky coincidence" of our having an English speaking physics teacher to converse with for several hours was a ploy by Yugoslav secret police, the State Security (UDBA) to gain information.

All we had was our faith in God to believe that our actions in Bucharest and the calamity with our van in Belgrade had not been discovered. We kept the conversation to what we had observed as differences in our cultures, the state of education in our different countries, and soccer versus football. His two companions, who spoke no English, conversed only with each other and did not engage in our conversation.

Valinka's grandmother opened the basket at her feet and proceeded to feed her grandchildren. Imagine our surprise when she offered her supplies to everyone in the compartment. Boiled potatoes, green peppers, and some kind of spiced meat were passed around.

She spoke no English, but I was deeply grateful for her generous spirit and thanked her profusely. We understood one another and she could tell that I was thankful for the lunch. We had not had time to purchase food for our long journey home.

I'm not sure we would have bought groceries even if we'd had time as I'd had no concept of how archaic the train would be. I must have thought we would be able to purchase food on the train. Not only was there no food service, we could not even move out of our compartment without stepping on someone.

I tried to give her money for the food since I had plenty *dinar* left, but she shook her head vehemently. I knew I had insulted her.

"*Poklon,*" Valinka said, extending her arms out with palms up. I caught that she meant the sharing of their food was a gift to us.

"*Hvala,*" I said, using the word for thank you I had learned from Officer Miroslav. I grabbed the old woman's hands. "*Hvala.*"

She nodded and seemed mollified. I had redeemed myself.

It wasn't long before we became very thirsty and uncomfortable. Although the friendly grandmother offered a goatskin bag of liquid that she was sharing with the others, I couldn't bring myself to drink from it. Lon went out into the hallway to see if he could reach the bathroom. He was gone for more than twenty minutes before he returned, shaking his head. Although he had found the restrooms, he informed me that it was not a healthy environment.

"Trust me," he said, "you don't want to go near it. It's so disgusting it made me retch. I went farther back, but it's even worse at the back of the train. Besides, you have to step over a lot of bodies to get to it, and I don't want you to go alone."

I took his word and decided the best idea was to catch some sleep. I dozed, listening to the sound of the train clacking on the tracks, and the buzz of foreign tongues conversing, singing, and arguing. My mind drifted to the faces of those wonderful people we had met: Our Christian brethren Nadia, Elika, Teodor and Elisabet, and Officer Miroslav, Mr. Petranovic, Valinka and her grandmother, and Buklev.

All throughout our journey we had met and been cared for by kind and generous strangers. My spirit felt an indescribable warmth. I drifted off into deep sleep. I was jolted awake by a screech of wheels as the train came to a halt.

"What's going on?" Lon asked Buklev.

"Border crossing. They will be checking our papers."

"Everyone? Everyone on the train?"

"Yes. Everyone."

It was true. The border guards fanned out into the train cars and picked their way through hundreds of bodies, examining everyone's passports and papers. It was an hour before a guard got to us. As we passed our passports to him, he stood in the doorway and scrutinized them. He looked at them with surprise. My heart nearly stopped when he turned and walked away with our passports in his hands.

"Why did he take our passports?" I asked Buklev.

He shrugged. "I don't know. Perhaps he has never seen American passports. You are a… how you say, a curious to them."

"A curiosity?"

He brightened. "Yes. You are a curiosity. You are not what we expect of Americans."

"What do you mean? How should we be?" I asked.

"We see Americans as tall people with big hats and much money. We would not expect you to ride on our trains."

I laughed. "Ah. I see. So you think Americans are not people like you."

"We see you as bigger than we are," Buklev said. "It is happy I am that I can tell people I know that you are nice people, just like us." He smiled broadly, and I nodded.

"Good," I said. "Please tell them we are all different: rich, poor, nice, mean, happy, sad, with troubles and dreams just like the Yugoslavians."

"I will tell them," Buklev said, "but Yugoslavia is not America."

I did not know what to say to that. I smiled in response.

Before long the guard returned with a companion. He pointed us out to the other guard. We smiled and said hello. They glared at us. Lon asked them if there was anything wrong, which only served to fluster them. Buklev spoke to them and they asked him a question.

"They want to know what you were doing in Romania."

"We've been traveling, camping in our van, but it broke down because we got bad gas in Romania. We had to take the train."

Buklev translated. The guard snorted, and I think I heard him say "Romania" derisively under his breath, but he seemed satisfied with the answer. He asked another question.

"Why did you go to Romania?"

"We are tourists," Lon said, sticking to the usual answer. "We wanted to see Bucharest and had hoped to drive all the way to the Black Sea and take the mud baths, but we ran out of time and had to return. Besides, my wife misses our children. Understand?"

Buklev translated our explanation to the guards, who seemed skeptical. Would they believe us or would they take us off the train and interrogate us. Finally, they decided we were telling the truth and handed us our passports. I nearly fainted with relief.

After another hour, the train jerked and began to move forward. One of Velinka's brothers began to squirm and complain. It was clear that the child needed to use the restroom. I was curious how grandmother would handle this?

She reached into her basket and came out with a towel, a spray bottle and a roll of toilet paper. She handed the toilet paper to the boy, put the towel and bottle under her arm, took the boy by the hand and moved out of the compartment and into the corridor. I was curious. I knew what she would be facing. Every available space was filled with people, sitting on the floor or leaning against the wall. I couldn't resist and got up to watch her progress. She chattered all along the corridor and people moved out of her way, moving their feet out of the way to make a space so that she and the boy could pass.

"You go with grandmother," Valinka said, blushing.

I was desperate to use the facilities and decided to risk it. I rushed after her. The corridor was still open and I made quick progress. I could smell the restroom before I got to it.

Grandmother pushed some people out of the way and opened the restroom door. I nearly fainted from the odor. Grandmother appeared unfazed. She instructed her grandson to stand still as she went in and began cleaning the toilet. When it was sanitary to her satisfaction, she pushed her grandson in and stood in front of the door. She saw me and gave me a toothless grin.

She beckoned me to her. Although I didn't exactly know what she said, I'm almost sure she was saying, "I am always prepared for the mess people make. It is clean now and you may go in after my grandson."

When the boy came out, she stepped aside, handed me the toilet paper roll and let me go in. The floor was not anything I wanted to look at, but the toilet seat was clean.

As I placed strips of paper down on the seat, I saw the ground rushing beneath the toilet bowl. It was an open hole to the tracks below. I sat and relieved myself. I was so grateful to grandmother. I would never have made it to Munich. I wished I could communicate with her because I wanted to know about her life. Given her age, she had lived through turbulent times and yet was able to keep her dignity, her gentleness, and her beauty of spirit. She had extended kindness to a stranger.

When I came out, she stepped in and shut the door. I waited for her with her grandson. When she came out, we picked our way back through the bodies on the floor to our compartment. When I arrived, Buklev and Lon were engaged in a conversation.

I could see by Buklev's face that he was talking about things that could get him into trouble. His voice was hushed and they leaned in toward each other and talked in low tones. Valinka was leaning forward trying to catch words from their conversation. Lon made room for me and I sat next to the door.

They resumed their conversation about the guest worker program, which accounted for reasons the trains were filled beyond capacity. According to Buklev, Yugoslavia was in an economic crisis. Growing unemployment had driven large numbers of workers to migrate to Western Europe. The government wholeheartedly supported the guest worker program because the money they brought back to Yugoslavia was mitigating the effects of the country's foreign debt and stagnant markets.

The new Yugoslavian Constitution of 1974 and the Law on Associated Labor of 1976 had reorganized the economy. Companies were dissolved into smaller enterprises called basic organizations of associated labor (BOALs). Workers now had more control.

This freedom was part of the reason why Yugoslavia appeared to be more democratic than its Eastern Bloc neighbors. There was a greater coordination between organized labor and the government. Although President Tito kept tight controls on intellectual and religious views, the economic situation introduced greater freedom for people to make money.

Buklev had great optimism for his country. As a physicist, he longed for the day he would be able to cross freely to other Western

European nations. His admiration for America was based on his belief that it stood for the best of man's intellectual freedom. I was only sorry we couldn't be more forthcoming.

Unfortunately for Buklev and the rest of the Yugoslavian people, this relatively idyllic peace between the citizens and its government was not to last. Tito had unified the six unique republics into a Communist dictatorship, independent of Russia.

Perhaps one of his greatest accomplishments for the unification of Yugoslavia was the suppression of religious and cultural rivalries among the Roman Catholics, Serbian Orthodox, and Muslims. In 1980, President Tito died, leaving a void of leadership that soon unraveled the unity he had created. Instead of choosing a strong leader, Yugoslavia created a collective leadership of the various republics.

During the 1980s, Yugoslavia suffered under a huge national debt and growing ethnic tensions. When Slobodan Milosevic became the Serbian Communist party leader in 1987, his overt nationalism greatly alarmed the other republics and each rushed to declare their independence.

In 1989, Serbia rescinded Kosovo's autonomy and sent in troops to suppress the largely Albanian population. After many attempts by Serbia to impose its rule on the rest of the country, fighting erupted and the entire region destabilized. War engulfed the region during the mid-1990s and terrible acts of genocide and mass murder occurred against the citizens of the region.

The world could no longer sit by and witness what was going on in the former Yugoslavia. The United Nations imposed economic sanctions on Serbia and Montenegro and called for an immediate cease-fire in Bosnia and Herzegovina. By 2003, after the war was over, the country of Yugoslavia was splintered into five sovereign states: Slovenia, Croatia, Bosnia Herzegovina, Serbia, and Macedonia.

Our time on the train was a rare glimpse of relative peace and unity in Yugoslavia. In our little compartment we had a mixture of generations, religions, nationalities, economies, education, and cultures, and yet we became friends, enjoying each other's company and helping each other survive the nightmare train ride.

When we arrived in Münich, Germany, we said goodbye to our new friends. We hugged, passed addresses, and watched them scatter in all directions, disappearing in the huge train station. The sound was deafening. Thousands of people milled around, rushing to catch their train, waiting for the next train, loitering for an opportunity to steal a wallet, meet a loved one, avoid a stalker; feeling exhausted, sad, in love, in grief. The sea of humanity took my breath away.

The difference was they lived in a democracy and were more or less free, free from the oppression of government scrutiny, the restriction of movement and assembly, the suppression of religion and different opinion. I knew the West wasn't perfect, but after traveling in two Communist countries and experiencing the pervasive fear of crossing a line that might lead to prison or death, I thanked God for America.

We had no trouble finding the train to Holland. Just seeing the well-maintained train made me choke up with gratitude. It would be a long trip, but we had our own sleeping compartment and that was a true luxury.

Through the night and into the day we traveled north through Germany, following the Rhine River. Sightseeing from the window of a train was a pleasant and satisfying experience. My eyes scrutinized the landscape. I squealed like a child every time I saw castles, which were plentiful along the Rhine. I felt so blessed and humbled by our situation. God had protected us all along the way, but even more so, He was seeing us safely home and had arranged for us to travel in style.

We got off the train in Amersfoort, Holland. We called the Shalom House and within fifteen minutes, Ryan showed up and drove us back. As we stepped out of the car, our children were waiting for us. We folded them into our arms and were pleased to see they were no worse for the separation. Our friends gathered around us and thanked God for our safe return.

A month later, our time had come to leave Holland. We left our Shalom House family and moved back to the United States. We picked up our car in New York City and took a month traveling across the states before seeing our families in Idaho and California.

Along the way, we spoke at many churches and civic groups about our trip behind the Iron Curtain, and the faith shown by the underground church. For many, the news of Christians living under such persecution came as a shock. We were thankful and touched that as we traveled westward hundreds of prayers went up to God asking for an end to the persecution of our brothers and sisters in Romania.

But we also became increasingly uncomfortable with what we found in many of the Bible-based churches in America. As we listened to sermons and talked to Christians across the country, we began to notice an unsettling shift in doctrine. It appeared to us that the American evangelical church was now gripped by a powerful "prosperity gospel," which equated faith with wealth or financial prosperity.

It was a very subtle change, and in a country of great prosperity and wealth, certainly understandable. It was particularly noticeable among the evangelical, charismatic and Pentecostal churches, promoted by Kenneth Hagin, Jim Bakker, and other televangelists; but we also found it in Bible and faith-based churches.

The scripture most often quoted was 3 John 2-4: "Beloved, I pray that you may prosper in all things and be in health, just as your soul prospers." In other words, God bestows prosperity upon those He favors. If you weren't prospering, you were not following God's will. God wanted you to be rich. Godliness appeared to be equated with positive balance sheets.

Since we had just come from a country where Christians lived under extreme persecution and in dire poverty but were willing to lay their lives on the line for their faith, the messages of prosperity rang hollow in our ears. We didn't understand where this new teaching was coming from but it made us extremely uncomfortable.

As our travels came to an end, we settled in Idaho near my parents, and attended the University of Idaho under the provisions of the GI

Bill. We started a Bible study group at school, but stayed away from the churches as we were uncomfortable with the new emphasis on prosperity. We spoke on occasion about our trip to Romania, but found it difficult to convey to churches that practiced the prosperity doctrine what the Romanian Christians were suffering.

I remember speaking one night at a church that had a large audience. When I finished my talk—moved by the retelling of the experience—the first question I got was from a man who wanted to know more about what kind of torture was being used on the Romanians. It wasn't the question so much as the look on his face that shocked me. He was titillated by evil.

I stammered, "I have no idea," and quickly took another question.

From then on I found it difficult to share our Bible smuggling experience. My husband and I became discouraged that our message of God's faithfulness and miraculous intervention on behalf of His church in Romania was not getting through to listeners.

Gradually we began refusing offers to speak and eventually stopped talking about our mission at all. For me, it was a sacred experience that I no longer wanted to share with people who were seeking entertainment. It was enough for me that God had used us to help His persecuted church. Personally experiencing the mighty hand of God is something never to be forgotten.

Years later after our trip, whenever I was confronted by difficulties or trials, I'd close my eyes and envision Elisabet's face, glowing with peace in the knowledge that the Good Shepherd was watching over His flock.

I would see the little white car from Morocco dismantled in front of us while we were being waved through an impenetrable border.

I would see the members of the underground church staring back at me and saying, "Do not be afraid. We see Jesus in your eyes."

I would see perfect strangers going above and beyond to help us like Officer Miroslav, Mr. Petranovic at the Ford Motor plant, and Velinka and her grandmother.

I would never forget the people we met or the joy I felt to answer the call.

# Epilogue

It was December 23, 1989. I was at home in southern California, humming Christmas carols as I prepared dinner for my family. I hoped the aroma of apple cider and cinnamon brewing on the stove mixed with the smells of succulent chicken cooking in the oven would lend a homey atmosphere and cause the men in my life to join me for dinner.

We were all such busy people. My two sons were in their last years of high school and so popular that it was difficult to compete for their attention. My husband was employed in the film industry and spent much of his time in Los Angeles. I never knew when he would make it home. I was a reporter at a local newspaper and sometimes had to cover a story after hours. Getting the family to sit down together for a meal was getting harder.

I could never get used to Christmas without snow, so I did my best to decorate the house with all the nostalgia accumulated from eighteen years of marriage.

Although the boys considered themselves grown up and didn't like sentimentality, they still expected a "traditional" Christmas. They insisted on putting up a "live" tree, decorating it together, and placing wooden *klopmens* under the tree, stuffed with grass and carrots for Sinterklass' white horse, *Sleipnir*, and chocolates for *Zwarte Piet*, Sinterklass' helper.

Another tradition that the boys insisted on was receiving a gift box filled with dirt. Ever since they were young children, it was rumored in our house that if they weren't good, their Christmas gifts could magically turn to dirt. Every year I found the perfect box to load with dirt. The one time I didn't follow this family tradition, they were disappointed, saying they were sure they were not that good.

I went into the living room and admired the Christmas tree in the corner. I loved the smell of freshly cut pine. It mixed nicely with the hot apple cider smell, wafting in from the kitchen. All our favorite ornaments hung on the branches, including the many we had brought back with us from Europe.

I carefully plucked off and admired one of the hand-blown crystal icicles that Meneer Van Asselt had given me when we lived in the Shalom House. What precious times, I thought. Twelve years had passed since we had lived in the Shalom House, where twenty of us sat down together every Saturday evening for a "love feast"— twelve years since the mission to Romania.

As I hung the crystal icicle in a better spot so that it dangled freely, I heard the word "Romania" coming from the television. I listened intently as the broadcaster announced that a revolution was occurring in Romania at that moment. I quickly turned up the volume and sat in front of the television.

The reporter was saying that although news was sketchy, it appeared that a full-blown revolution was underway in Romania, one of the last of the hardline Communist countries. Romanian President Nicolae Ceausescu and his wife, Elena, had fled the capital city of Bucharest. I watched as shaky video images showed huge crowds in the central square, chanting "Timisoara, Timisoara!"

The reporter stated that this was a reference to one of Romania's largest cities, about five hundred miles from Bucharest, that had been experiencing unrest and appeared to be the catalyst of the revolution. He went on to say that on December 16, a protest had broken out in Timisoara. It began when the government had tried to remove a dissident clergyman from his church for preaching anti-Communist sermons.[9]

According to the report, hundreds of church members barred the way of the local police and Securitate as they tried to remove Pastor Laszlo Tokes by force. The crowd grew in size, filling the streets in front of the church. Soon hundreds of people outside were chanting anti-Communist slogans. The crowd grew larger.

Desperate to end the uprising, the mayor of Timisoara rescinded the order to evict Tokes from his church, but the damage was already done. The crowds refused to disperse. Martial law was declared, people defied it, and some were killed. This further enraged the people of Timisoara. Workers refused to go back to their jobs. A general strike was called and commerce came to a halt.

I sat with rapt attention, watching the surprising video of Pastor Lazlo Tokes, a tall, gaunt man in a black cassock waving a Bible, using it to punctuate what he was saying to a massive crowd. I caught my breath; my eyes glued onto the Bible in his hand.

I would know it anywhere since I had pulled five thousand of them out of a custom-made smuggler's van. Could it be one of them? If not, it was similar in every way; same size, same thickness, same cover. My body shook with the certainty that our mission was now bearing fruit in an unexpected way. I got down on my knees and thanked God. Something extraordinary was happening in Romania—freedom was coming!

Over the next few years, information trickled out of Romania as to what had happened. Since the Revolution of 1989, most sources agreed that Pastor Lazlo Tokes' defiance; his standing up for truth, had served as the catalyst for the revolution.

From his church in Timisoara, the spirit of resistance spread to the people in the streets and to the workers. Their demonstration shut down the city. Riots and protests escalated. The growing unrest eventually spread to Bucharest. Massive numbers of workers flooded the capital city on a frigid winter's day, December 21, 1989.

From the balcony of the Central Committee building, President Ceausescu addressed a huge crowd of workers, students, and citizens. His speech started with the usual Communist slogans and propaganda. He went on to condemn the uprising in Timisoara.

As is always the case with despots, he had no idea as to the crowd's ugly mood. Only a few minutes into his speech, they began to jeer him and chant, "Timisoara, Timisoara!" Without warning, gunfire erupted and the crowd panicked. Chaos ensued (to this day there is a dispute as to which side fired first).

Soldiers, Securitate, and tanks confronted the unarmed protesters. Since the president's speech was being broadcast live throughout Romania, the entire country witnessed the people demonstrating, the tanks firing on unarmed protesters, and their president scurrying back into the building as the city erupted in chaos. The spirit of revolution was ignited.[10]

According to news reports, hundreds of thousands of people fought back against the police and Securitate. Many soldiers and police deserted their ranks and joined the revolution. The Ceausescus left their presidential palace and fled Bucharest in a helicopter. Later testimonies stated that the helicopter pilot pretended to be experiencing problems and set down in a field near Pitesti.

Alone in a field with no other transportation available, the fleeing Ceausescus and their two Securitate officers flagged down two cars. The driver of the car who was transporting Nicolae and Elena Ceausescu pretended to have engine trouble and pulled over. Unable to go any farther, the Ceausescus flagged down another car. This driver drove them to Targoviste. He persuaded them to hide in a room in a building. When they followed his advice, he locked them in. The local police arrived and found the once all-powerful Ceausescus hiding in a closet.

Nicolae and Elena Ceausescu were later tried, convicted and executed by firing squad on Christmas Day, 1989. The revolutionary war continued until December 27 when it abruptly stopped. About fifteen hundred people lost their lives during the revolution, but the country was finally free of Communist rule. In 1991, Romania established a democracy with basic freedoms.

The U.S. State Department's most recent report on Romania is astounding and demonstrates the incredible change that has taken place in one of the most ruthless and oppressive regimes behind the Iron Curtain. The report is as follows:

> "Romania's 1991 constitution proclaims Romania a democracy and market economy, in which human dignity, civic rights, and freedoms, the unhindered development of human personality, justice, and political pluralism are supreme and guaranteed values.

> "The 1996 local elections demonstrated a major shift in the political orientation of the Romanian electorate... The campaign of the opposition hammered away on the twin themes of the need to squelch corruption and to launch economic reform. The message resonated with the electorate, which swept Emil Constantinescu and parties allied to him to power in free and fair presidential and parliamentary elections.

> "Romania acceded to the European Union on January 1, 2007, along with Bulgaria, bring-

ing the number of EU states to twenty-seven.
Romania is a strong advocate for a "larger
Europe," encouraging other countries that were
formerly part of the Soviet sphere to integrate
into both NATO and the EU. Romania hosted
President Bush's final NATO Summit April 2-4,
2008. The venue symbolized the expansion of
the Alliance from the Baltic to the Black Sea
and set new goals for years to come.

"Romania maintains good diplomatic relations
with Israel and was supportive of the Middle
East peace negotiations initiated after the Gulf
conflict in 1991."[11]

Although the first freely elected President of Romania, Dr. Emil
Constantinescu, did not seek re-election, he continues to be a strong
voice for democratic principles and human rights in Romania.
When my husband and I went to Romania in 1977, we were foiled
in our attempt to meet our contact whom we knew only as Dr.
Constantinescu. I cannot say for certain that these two men are the
same man. However, I did come across an article that stated the
former Romanian president and his wife, Nadia, continue to live
in Bucharest.

*Remember me. Nadia Constantinescu.*

We will never really know how big an impact our mission to
Romania had on ensuing events, but I believe that we played a part

in bringing to an end the cruel regime of a Communist dictator.

I cannot help but think that as we live in freedom in the United States, we often take for granted our right to assemble, to voice dissent, to practice our faith, and to govern ourselves. In a relatively short period of time, the people of Yugoslavia and Romania fell under Communist rule and that which they had taken for granted was lost to them. No matter how sophisticated we become, we need to thank God for the freedoms we enjoy.

Through the faith and courage of Christian believers everywhere— willing to lay their lives on the line to spread the good news of a living God who forgives and longs for a personal relationship with His creation through the redemption of Jesus Christ—mighty, seemingly omnipotent, rulers are cast down.

Those who sneer and devalue the power of Christianity in the world have never suffered under the rule of a godless state. The power of God to intercede in human events through the prayers of the believers is as real today as it was when Moses obeyed his call and led the children of Israel out of Egypt.

We were called to take Bibles to the Romanian Christians. God used us to answer the prayers of the persecuted church. Through the many miraculous occurrences of our trip, we were assured that it was not by our minds, our will or our good fortune that we succeeded. God was in control. I believe as much today as I did while I was in the midst of our mission that God was leading us and kept us from harm in the palm of His hand.

For those who believe, you can be assured that God has you in the palm of His hand. Here you can be at peace and not fear the troubles and terrors of the day. If you have willfully jumped from His hand, know that He is still with you and longs for your return.

For those of you who have never experienced the hand of God on your life, if you believe in Him and ask forgiveness through Jesus Christ, He will answer you, hold you in His hands, and never let you go—even to the end of time.

# Afterword

I was born into the Christian faith, but I did not actually become a Christian until January 11, 1971, when I accepted Jesus Christ as my Savior. This transformed me. I then lived in the bubble of His love, unfazed by anything that came my way. I lived my life by faith. In fact, I lived entirely on faith that God would provide. And God provided; many times. For those who believe, God is faithful.

It is with great humility that I tell you that even though God revealed Himself to me over and over again through answered prayer and miracles, I lost faith because of a great grief that struck my life. After the Romanian Revolution of 1989, a revolution occurred in my own home.

My twenty-year marriage dissolved in 1992. My reaction to that blow was not to plunge myself deeper into God's loving and merciful arms but to become angry. I had a monumental temper tantrum that lasted for decades. I was so mad at God that I chose to put my faith in my intelligence, my beauty, my personality, and my stubborn German perseverance. I would control my own destiny and make my own successes. This was a monumental mistake. I did no better for myself; in fact, I replaced my former peace and joy with heartache, uncertainty, and anxiety. Happiness was as elusive as the desires of my heart.

Until God stopped me in my tracks.

My life now is a testament that God loves us and will not forsake us, no matter how willful we are or the length of our temper tantrum. Here I was, at the top of my career, excelling in a position that was made for me, when I was abruptly and without explanation let go—just in time to enter the economic downturn and the flood of unemployed.

As with many people, I had followed all the rules for success. I worked hard, took every opportunity to improve myself, and played by all the rules. I was very good at what I did. I was a good person, practiced kindness and honesty, and nurtured a child-like innocence. It was important for me not to let the disappointments of my life take away what I thought were my best qualities.

Even though I was mad at God, I still trusted Him to protect me and guide me through my life. But it was a hollow faith. I had relegated God to the back seat. I was in the driver's seat. I didn't see the crash coming until it was too late.

It was a shock to the system. How? How had this happened? Everything I had worked for, strived and sacrificed for, all my plans and security, were ripped away from me in an instant. As I neared retirement, my retirement funds drained away in the economic meltdown. As a single woman, I was on my own. Fear reared up and paralyzed me.

I know I'm not alone. There are millions out there who had the same rude awakening that I had. The shock and dismay at this occurrence drove me to question my reality, what beliefs I was living by. Once I started going down that road, I couldn't turn back. The questions grew more and more introspective. What had gone wrong? What had I done wrong? What was I to do now? What was important to me? What had happened to my dreams? And the ultimate question—Was I happy? These questions plagued me night and day. Where would I find the answers? I was without resources, without a plan, and without answers. I was at my wit's end.

As I paced the floor of my bedroom, shouting these questions into the air, my gut aching and my mind racing, my hands clasped, begging for an answer to my dilemma, I heard a voice.

*Trust and follow me.*

"What?" I stopped dead in my tracks. "What was that?"

I waited expectantly for the supernatural voice to speak again. Nothing. Did I hear something? Did I imagine it? I thought I had heard something.

"Was that you, God? Are you talking to me?" I waited. Nothing. I stopped pacing and dropped to my knees. "If that is you, God, I need to hear from you. Please speak to me!"

I closed my eyes. I stilled all the questions in my head. I waited expectantly.

*You are in the palm of my hand. I will not let you fall. Trust and follow me.*

I heard the words inside me. It wasn't an external voice, but it rang clear in my ears, nonetheless. Tears welled up from deep within and flowed down my face. I remembered those words. They had been spoken to me before a long time ago.

*Though your path ahead will be hard, you will not walk alone for I will be with you. Trust and follow me.*

My body shook with the subtle revelation that I wasn't alone. God was still with me. I felt pain, grief, and fear leave my body. I was different. From then on, I put all my trust in God. My problems were still there, but they were diminished by the knowledge that God would not let me fall.

This experience left me open to watch for the hand of God in my life. I looked for blessings and I found them. Most importantly, my unemployment allowed me to spend quality time with my youngest grown son, Eli, his wife, and two children. Pursuing a career had taken me far away from him, so I was thankful for every moment I had with him as we renewed our bond and reveled in our time together.

On one of these occasions, he told me that he had met a relative from the other side of the family. This man was elderly and a little confused. He mistook him for his father.

"We were all praying for you when you were smuggling those Bibles," he said, clamping a hand on my son's shoulder. "We knew

God would be faithful and I'm glad to see you made it." There was a little awkwardness as family members intervened and explained whom he was talking to, but my son couldn't get it out of his head.

"What did he mean? What was he talking about?" he asked me.

The memories came flooding back. I told him his father and I had smuggled Bibles behind the Iron Curtain when he was a little boy. He wanted to know more, but I couldn't talk about it then. I hadn't thought about it for years. But, from then on the memories of that miraculous journey were brought forward to my conscious mind.

As I thought about it, I was reminded of how faithful God had been. I remembered many miracles that happened before and after that journey. My own faith was renewed. The hand of God was again in my life. I learned that a generous, merciful God leaves a thousand sheep to fetch the one who has stupidly wandered away.

From that point on, I was consumed by an urgent need to chronicle my Bible smuggling trip to Romania. I felt the hand of God guiding me as I wrote. It was imperative that my children and grandchildren know how God had cleared our path to bring Bibles to the underground church in Romania.

Every day and sometimes through the night, I wrote. When I finished the story, I gave copies to my sons, Eli and Nathan, so that they would know that God is real and acting in human lives. Little did I realize, that the urgency I felt was because of a greater purpose.

Four months after I delivered the story to my sons, I received a call in the early morning hours to tell me that my precious thirty-six-year-old son, Eli, was dead. He was in Switzerland finishing a movie on his lifelong passion—skydiving—when Death snatched him from the sky. The news was devastating. Not only to me, to his brother, and to his father, but to his two young daughters and his wife, who was nine months pregnant with their first son.

Nothing can prepare you for the death of a child of any age. Nothing can possibly be worse. But I had given my life to God. He was my Center. So this time, although facing horrific grief and devastation, I didn't blame God or rail against him. I didn't send Him to the back seat so that I could drive. I lay on my bed and cried out to Him for solace in the depths of my cavern of pain.

"God, oh God, help me endure this pain!"

Before my eyes, a shimmering white box descended from the ceiling and settled over all four sides of my bed. I know I was not dreaming because immediately my gut-wrenching sobs ceased. I was filled with a peace that bears no description. The pain was completely gone. An assurance of God's infinite love infused my being.

"This is a provision of God," I thought. "A gift box to me from my Creator."

I lay still. I didn't dare move. I didn't want to disturb something so precious and so desperately needed. My heart was covered with a balm that eased the agonizing ache. I knew that God was present and in control. I was no longer alone. He was with me in a real, tangible way, showing me His mercy and His love.

Eventually, I got out of bed, moved through the shimmering walls, and walked outside into the night. The stars were shining brightly in a midnight sky. I carried His serenity and peace with me as I wandered in the backyard, looking up at the sky. The majesty and beauty of God's creation filled me with praise and worship.

I saw myself through God's eyes—a tiny precious light. Within my spirit, I heard His voice: "Even as you walk through this valley of death, fear not, for I am with you. And Eli is with me."

I can't pretend that enduring the death of my son has been easy. But always, God comforts me and brings me peace. I am so thankful that I was able to put this story in his hands before he went to be with the Lord. I believe it was instrumental in helping him find his way home.

It is my hope that it will also lead others to acknowledge the mighty unseen hand of God in their lives if they trust and follow Him. This is what He says to you:

*Have no fear. I have you in the palm of my hand. Follow me and nothing will harm you.*

**Shalom House, Leusden, Holland
(for height perspective, note the cars on the right)**

**The author at a campground outside Salzburg, Austria.**

The Yugoslavian border at the top of the Wurzenpaß.

Driving down the pass in Yugoslavia, oxen impede our progress.

One of the beautiful city centers in Yugoslavia.

Near the Romanian border are endless fields of sunflowers.

**The unfortunate white car in front of us at the Romanian border.**

**Women carry a heavy load in Romania.**

A sure sign that we are on the right road to Bucharest.

Our first view of the capital city of Bucharest.

**The Arcul de Triumf at the center of Bucharest.**

**Our campground in Bucharest.**

The red and white tram we used to find our contact.

Risking a photo of the Romanian border, we depart safely.

One of many gypsy camps in Yugoslavia.

The train station in Zagreb, Yugoslavia.

# References

[1] Open Doors International, Brother Andrews website: www.opendoorsusa.org

[2] Ten Boom, Corrie and Sherrill, John and Elizabeth; *The Hiding Place* (*"De Schuilplaats"*), Chosen Books; Fleming H. Revell Co., 1971)

[3] Corrie Ten Boom website: www.corrietenboom.com

[4] Andrew, Brother; *God's Smuggler,* Baker Publishing Group, Grand Rapids, MI. 2001.

[5] *Encyclopedia Britannica*, 14th Edition, 1973.

[6] The Voice of the Martyrs: www.persecution.com

[7] Wurmbrand, Richard; *Tortured for Christ*, Living Sacrifice Book Co., 1998.

[8] *The Europa World Year Book*, Vol. 2, Routledge Taylor & Francis Group, London, New York, 2008.

[9] Tokes, Laszlo; *The Fall of Tyrants: The Incredible Story of One Pastor's Witness, the People of Romania and the Overthrow of Ceausescu,* Good News Publishing, 1991.

[10] Ion Mihai Pacepa; Red Horizons: *The True Story of Nicolae and Elena Ceausescus' Crimes, Lifestyle, and Corruption*, published in the U.S. by Regnery Gateway, 1987.

[11] U.S. Department of State, Bureau of Public Affairs, Publications Office, Background on Romania.

# About the Author

Deborah Kaine Thompson became a follower of Christ through the 'Jesus Movement' in 1971 and began using her writing talent to spread the Gospel and encourage and empower women disciples.

She currently teaches writing at the university level and is a book editor and inspirational speaker. Covering crime and city government, she previously worked as a reporter for two California newspapers. She later established a successful career in higher education as a public relations professional. She holds a master's degree in writing from California State University, Northridge and a bachelor's degree from University of Oregon.

Deborah is the author of several books, including *Remember Her For This: A Study on the Women of the Gospels,* a 2017 Silver Illumination Book Award, and two works of Christian literary fiction: *When Gods Collide* and *The Living Stones*.

She lives in Mesa, Arizona where she serves as chaplain for a community church.

~ ~ ~ ~ ~

Made in the USA
Columbia, SC
04 April 2022

58473767R00140